MIRACLES AND GRACE IN AN UNLIKELY PLACE

Memoir of a Christian Woman
Biker-Bar Owner

By
Ms. Charisse A. Tyson

Copyright © 2013 Ms. Charisse A. Tyson

All rights reserved.

ISBN: 0988924404

ISBN 13:   9780988924406

Library of Congress Control Number: 2013901634
Lifeanew Publishing
Hollister, California

For my loving husband whose unwavering faith that I can accomplish anything I put my mind to encouraged me to stay the course. Thank you for allowing me to share our story. My prayer is that readers dealing with addictions and co-dependency will find hope between these pages.

CONTENTS

FOREWORD ix
INTRODUCTION 1

SHOCK AND CONFUSION
My Life Is Turned Upside Down   6

OPENING MY HEART TO AN ALCOHOLIC
A Whirlwind Beginning   10
I Had a History; Therapy Helped   15

FAST, TUMULTUOUS, PAINFUL, WONDERFUL
Hollister — Our New Home   22
At Last: Married!   27
Teenage Rebellion, Job Turmoil, and Psychotherapy   29

A YEAR OF FIRSTS
Johnny's - Opportunity Knocks   34
Charisse Tyson: Bar Owner   40
The Grand Opening—Enter Jeana   50
Saint Patrick's Day, 1996   53
Tough Love Ain't Easy   59
Tommy Probably Shouldn't Tend Bar   60
The Bike Blessing of 1996   66
Karaoke: A Tradition Begins   72

OUR HISTORIC SIGNIFICANCE —PARADES AND RALLIES

The Wild One Put Johnny's
on the Map   79

1996 Our First Rodeo Parade   82

What Really Happened in Hollister In 1947?   85

The Inception of Our Rally   89

The Dry Run Rally of 1996   91

Lights on Parade—A Float,
Are You Crazy?   94

BUSINESS BOOMING AND I'M LEARNING

Rodeo Parade, June 1997   102

July 1997: The Fiftieth Anniversary Motorcycle Rally   104

CLAMPERS, WIDDERS, & TRIATHLONS

What Say the Brethren? Satisfactory!   123

The Widders' Ball   126

The Johnny's Triathlon Begins   128

KIDS, KIDNEY STONES, AND BIG SURPRISES

Kat With a K Saves the Day   134

Miss Sylvia   136

Enter Woo   137

What Do You Mean, You Don't Own a Motorcycle?   139

LIFE WAS A PARTY; THEN I WOKE UP

Ignoring the Problem in Front of My Face   146

A Disintegrating Marriage and a Warped Mind   150

THE D-WORD, AL-ANON, HEALING, AND GRACE
This Can't Be Happening to Me   156
Trying to Find My Balance   167
Light at the End of the Tunnel   175
Healing for My Mind, Body, and Spirit   179
Praying and Believing   185

THE ONLY WAY OUT IS TO GO THROUGH
Trying to Do It God's Way— No One Said It Was Going to Be Easy   190
I Told You Not to Make Them Angry   193
Am I Finally Getting a Break?   200
Daytona Bike Week, 2004   208

RECOVERY- WE'RE JUST GETTING STARTED
Mowing Down Mailboxes   212
The Camp Recovery Center   215
Sobriety and an Award- It Doesn't Get Much Better Than That   220
Alcoholics Anonymous and God   225

GUARDIAN ANGELS EVERYWHERE
Help Me, Lord; It's Thursday   228
His Timing, Not Mine   233
An Intervention   236

SURVIVING ANOTHER ROUGH PATCH
As the Kitchen Turns   242
The Un-rally of 2006   245
Kitchen Still Spinning   253
The Hollister Motorcycle
Rally Committee   257
Road Trip—The Sturgis Investigation   260
The 2007 and 2008 Hollister Motorcycle Rallies   270

STILL GROWING
Trust and Mouth Issues Continue   278
New Beginnings   283
EPILOGUE   285
Acknowledgements   287

FOREWORD

Praise for Miracles and Grace in an Unlikely Place

Charisse Tyson is a remarkable lady.

I met Charisse several years ago on my first trip to Hollister. At Johnny's Bar, of course.

Bill Hayes, my life-love-and-business partner who brought me there, is the Press and Publicity Officer for the Boozefighters Motorcycle Club as well as the author of the bestselling book about them, *The Original Wild Ones: Tales of the Boozefighters Motorcycle Club*. The long term connection between Johnny's and the club is well chronicled in it.

The passion of my life is empowering women. As a fourth-degree black belt and co-owner of a karate studio, I do everything in my power to spread strength and confidence to other women. And in meeting Charisse, I surmised that she must also be an "empowered" woman. Boy, was I right.

It takes incredible bravery and strength to do what Charisse has done. To react to a dysfunctional relationship by truly looking inward. To examine one's own role in a situation and strive to heal oneself instead of continually trying to fix others. Very few people do that. Placing blame is so much easier.

It's through her own emotional healing that Charisse has been able to help so many others. She has spread God's healing light not only to her husband, but to her friends, to her bar patrons, and now to her readers.

Thank you, Charisse, for having the courage and tenacity to heal your soul and for sharing your journey with us.

Jennifer Thomas, Editor-in-Chief, *Butterfly Tears: Stories of Entrapment to Empowerment;* Co-owner & instructor, Old School Kenpo Karate.

INTRODUCTION

My name is Charisse Tyson; my friends call me Cat. I'm a Christian woman married to a recovering alcoholic, and I own the famous biker bar *Johnny's Bar & Grill* in Hollister, California. My husband's name is Tommy. We met and became inseparable in 1989 and were married in 1993. By the grace of God, Tommy found sobriety on November 5, 2005, and he is still sober today.

When I bought Johnny's in December of 1995, I knew that it had been a favorite watering hole for farmers, businessmen, and local politicians for more than fifty years, but I didn't realize I'd purchased a bar with unprecedented historical significance.

Bartending is in my blood. I was managing a bar by the time I was nineteen years old, good at it, I might add—so when the opportunity to make the dream of owning my own place presented itself, I bought Johnny's. Soon after the purchase, I found out the bar was the center of the infamous motorcyclists' riot that took place in Hollister over the July Fourth weekend in 1947. Reportedly, four thousand motorcyclists took over the tiny town and put it and my bar on the map. Six years later, the 1953 film based on the incident, *The Wild One*, starring Marlon Brando, changed the perception of motorcyclists forever.

From 1947 on, seasoned motorcyclists from all over the world have been making the trek to historic Johnny's for a beverage, a burger, and a good time with great camaraderie.

In retrospect, buying a bar while knowing full well that my husband, the man I adored, was a practicing alcoholic was not the wisest move I'd ever made. I believe that there is a purpose for everything that happens in life, and God's watchful eyes never left me, even when I was ignoring Him completely.

Johnny's quickly became the "Cheers" of Hollister, and I thoroughly enjoyed the parties, road trips, and friendships the bar afforded us. It's just that where I could draw a line between partying and running my business, my husband could not. I learned many lessons the hard way, but it gave me the story that I now have to share with you.

In *Miracles & Grace in an Unlikely Place,* I hope to take you on the journey of a codependent, control-freak wife, my alcoholic husband, and my reconnection to God, all taking place while I ran a historic bar filled with a rich history that I'll also be sharing within these pages. For privacy reasons, some names were changed, but the story I'm telling you in *Miracles & Grace in an Unlikely Place* is all true.

I've spent a third of my life running this renowned little bar called Johnny's Bar & Grill in Hollister, California, and my many experiences running Johnny's give credence to this article of faith: God will use you right where you are.

I've been called a hypocrite. "How can you run a bar and call yourself a Christian?" they ask. Jesus said it best in Matthew 9:10–12: *"That night Matthew invited Jesus and his disciples to be his dinner guests, along with his fellow tax collectors and many other notorious sinners. The Pharisees were indignant. "Why does your teacher eat with such scum?" they asked his disciples. When he heard this Jesus replied, "Healthy people don't need a doctor—sick people do." Then He added, "Now go and learn the meaning of this scripture: I want you to be merciful; I don't want your sacrifices. For I have come to call sinners, not the self-righteous back to God."*

SHOCK AND CONFUSION

MY LIFE IS TURNED UPSIDE DOWN

The room spun. My head pounded. *This isn't happening. I must have heard wrong.*

Finally, Dr. Sullivan broke the silence. "Tom, are you saying that you don't want to try to work things out with Charisse?"

"I'm saying it's no use. I'll never be good enough for her no matter how hard I try."

"Try?" I all but screamed. "You must be kidding! You drink a bottle of vodka and Jack Daniel's every day, and drive around risking everything we've built while I pay all of the bills. I'm constantly scared to death that you're going to get hurt or be arrested. Try?"

Tommy stood up. "What's the use? I'll meet you in the car." He walked out of the office and slammed the door behind him.

I looked at Dr. Sullivan. "What just happened?"

"It's clear that your husband has no intention of giving up alcohol. He doesn't seem interested in saving your marriage, either. I suggest you stay in therapy and get yourself to an Al-Anon meeting as soon as possible, Ms. Tyson. You need to face the fact that your husband will probably always put alcohol before you and your relationship."

My Life Is Turned Upside Down

Those words landed like a gut punch from Muhammad Ali. Though I'd told myself the same thing many times, hearing it vocalized from this guy who didn't know me from Adam was demoralizing.

Then Dr. Sullivan gave me some Al-Anon brochures, made an appointment for me to see him the following week, and walked me to the door.

As I was leaving the office, he told me, "You're a strong woman, and I'm sure that you are going to be just fine. Get yourself to one of those meetings as soon as you can, and I'll see you next week."

The therapist's office was in downtown Monterey on the second floor of an old Victorian building. I hadn't noticed how narrow the staircase was on the way up, but my claustrophobia kicked into high gear by the time I walked down. It took an eternity to get to the door, and by then I was hyperventilating. I needed to get outside quick. When I did, I couldn't find the car. Where did we park? I was crying so hard that I could barely see through my tears. Finally I spotted Tommy sitting in my Durango across the street about half a block away. My feet felt like they weighed fifty pounds each as I dragged myself to the car. I got in and we drove in silence for a long time. Finally the dam broke.

"What do you mean, it's no use?" I asked.

"Just what I said: This marriage hasn't been working for a long time. You'll be much better off without me. You are a good person and you deserve better."

He said it so matter-of-factly, like it was something that he had been considering for a long time. How did I not see this coming?

"We have our first visit to the marriage counselor and you announce that you want to split up?" I couldn't bring myself to say the D-word. I was sobbing so hard that I could barely get the words out.

"I don't know what more to tell you, Charisse."

It's crazy how a little thing like your name can feel like a slap in the face. When I was mad, my husband was Tommy; when I was livid he was Thomas. I had been using his name quite a bit lately, but I hadn't heard him use mine in years. His face was emotionless. He turned on the radio to drown out my sobbing. Tammy Wynette was singing, "Stand by Your Man." To my relief, he changed the station quickly. "Bad Moon Rising" was not much better, but a rock station was an improvement. It was one of the longest rides of my life.

OPENING MY HEART TO AN ALCOHOLIC

A WHIRLWIND BEGINNING

I met Tommy in October of 1989 at a little bar where I worked as a cocktail waitress on Friday nights. Though I had a full-time job at a company delivering potato chips, I kept my hand in the bar business. The extra cash was great, and I loved being with the customers. I am a people person in every sense of the word.

The bartender I worked with told me about a nice-looking man who had been stopping in regularly for a couple of drinks on his way home from work. She said he seemed like a real nice guy, and told me that if she weren't married, she'd give him her telephone number.

The Friday night that Tommy came through the door, I knew immediately he was the man she had been talking about. He was tall and clean-cut and wore a blue uniform. My mama always said I was a sucker for a man in a uniform, from a fireman to a garbage man. Though her "garbage man" crack wasn't very nice, she had a point.

Tommy sat down at a table and I sauntered over to see what he wanted to drink. It was pretty quiet, so when I brought him his Korbel and water, I hung around and visited for a while. We hit it off right away. He was easy to talk to and we had a lot in common. When he asked whether I was spoken for, I said I was "semi-spoken for." I told him I had been dating a man, off and on, for eleven years who was commitment-phobic. I wanted him to know that despite having settled into a pretty comfortable relationship, I kept my options open.

"How about if I give you my number, and you can call me if you want to get together?" Tommy said. He wrote his number on a beverage napkin with the words, *Not semi-spoken for*, and put it on my tip tray.

The following Friday night he didn't stop by, so toward the end of my shift, I called him. He seemed a little stunned to hear from me. I asked whether he wanted to meet for a drink when I got off work.

"I don't usually go out of the house at this hour," he said.

"That's all right. We can do it another time."

"I'm not ready for bed, but I've got sweats on. I can throw on some clothes. Where do you want to meet?"

We agreed to meet at a bar halfway between our houses. It had been a while since I'd been there, and I knew a couple of the bartenders. It would be nice to see them again.

I hung up the phone and chuckled to myself. He sure did backpedal when I said we could do it another time. I took that as a good sign. I got to the bar ahead of him and ordered a beer from my pal Freddy. I no sooner took a sip than Tommy was at my side.

"Hi, there," I said. "You look pretty nice for a guy who was in sweats thirty minutes ago." He wore a cream-colored shirt and dark blue slacks. His sandy brown hair had a hint of red in it that complemented his hazel eyes.

"Tommy, this is my friend Freddy. What would you like to drink, a Korbel and water?"

"You're having a beer. I think I'll just have a Bud Light."

"Great. Fix up my friend, will you, Freddy?"

The band at the bar was great. When we weren't dancing, we were gabbing away. The music was loud and we had to move in close to hear each other talk, but neither one of us minded a bit. Before we knew it, Freddy yelled for last call.

"Man, the night flew by. I haven't enjoyed myself this much in a long time," I said. Tommy agreed.

By then, he'd told me about a wedding he was attending the next day. As we were leaving, he said, "I wish I didn't have to go to that darn wedding, because I'd love to get together again."

"You said the wedding wasn't until two o'clock. Why don't we meet for brunch at El Torito's before you go?"

"That sounds great. I'll meet you there at about eleven, if that works for you."

"Eleven will be perfect."

With our plans locked up for the next day, Tommy walked me to my car. I wanted to avoid the awkward good-night kiss, so I stood on my tiptoes and planted a quick peck on his lips. "I'll see you tomorrow," I said, and got into my car. I was grinning like a Cheshire cat all the way home. I couldn't remember ever being that comfortable with a man I hardly knew. I found myself thinking, *He could be the one.*

* * *

I went to bed with a smile on my face and slept like a baby. The next morning I took special care in getting ready for our second date. My pattern was to get into relationships too quickly, but something felt different this time. With the help of therapy, I felt equipped for a healthy relationship, and I was definitely ready for one.

I arrived at the restaurant a little early and picked a quiet table where we could talk. Tommy looked great. He had on black slacks and a light blue dress shirt. Darn, he was a handsome man.

"I thought I'd wait for you to order a drink, in case you wanted the champagne that comes with brunch," I said.

"I'll have the champagne with brunch, but I'd really like to start with a screwdriver. I don't usually stay up that late, and my head's a little fuzzy."

"Great. I'll have a Bloody Mary."

We laughed and shared funny stories about our lives, and before we knew it, it was time for Tommy to leave for the wedding.

A Whirlwind Beginning

"What are you doing tomorrow?" he asked.

"I'm planning on watching the 49ers game. If you'd like, come by my place and I'll fix us some breakfast. We can watch the game together. I have to pick up my son from his dad's in Concord at about five, but I'm free till then."

"Sounds wonderful; give me directions to your house and I'll see you at about ten."

With that he was off, and I headed home to do some serious housecleaning. As a kid, I was the one in charge of keeping the house clean, so I rebelled as an adult and developed a bad habit of not putting things away. If I wasn't expecting company, my place was pretty much in a state of disarray.

Once home, I worked diligently to make sure the duplex was pristine. I wanted to make a good impression. I went to the grocery store and filled my cart with everything I needed for our day of football together. My menu included a bacon, scallion, and white cheddar frittata with fried potatoes accompanied by champagne and orange juice for breakfast. For snacks during the second game, I had salami, ham, and Swiss and sharp cheddar cheeses, along with apples, grapes, cantaloupe, and crackers. I made sure I had plenty of beer. I was well prepared for our third date in as many days.

* * *

At nine fifty-five the next morning, Tommy arrived with a twelve-pack of beer, a bottle of vodka, a carton of orange juice, and some pastries.

"You didn't have to bring all this. Today was my treat," I said.

"I didn't want to show up empty-handed."

"Well, come on in. Breakfast is ready."

"Something smells delicious."

"The game is about to start. Have a seat and I'll get the food on the table. How about some champagne and orange juice, or would you rather I fix you a screwdriver?"

"I'll have a mimosa with you."

I prepared us both a plate and joined Tommy at the table. We clinked glasses and toasted to new friends.

"This breakfast is wonderful. I think I hit the jackpot: a feisty, nonsmoking redhead who knows how to cook and loves watching the 49ers on Sunday. What more could a guy ask for?"

"You are one lucky guy," I said with a wink.

We yelled and screamed at the television set and played a little kissy-face, too. I don't remember whether the 49ers won or who played the second game, but we were having such a nice time, I hated to see it end. At three thirty the phone rang, and it was my son Allen's father confirming his pickup time.

"I could go along with you if you'd like," Tommy said.

"That would be great. I hate making the long ride alone."

We talked the entire trip and the ninety-minute drive flew by. We never seemed to run out of things to say to each other. It was the most unpretentious and comfortable relationship I had ever experienced. We'd been at the gas station where I usually picked up Allen for about five minutes when he and his father arrived. I made introductions, Allen got into the car, and we headed back to San Jose. Tommy and Allen hit it off right away. He kept my son engaged in conversation all the way home. When we got back to my place, Tommy thanked me for a wonderful day and got ready to head home.

"You don't have to leave right away," I said.

"I've got to get up early for work, and Allen hasn't seen you all weekend, so I'm going to get going."

"You don't have to go," Allen, piped in.

"Thanks a lot, but it's getting late. I'd better be going."

I gave Tommy a kiss good night, and when he said, "I'll call you tomorrow," I knew he meant it. He didn't even wait until the next day. When he got home, he called to tell me what a great time he'd had. I felt like a teenager with her first crush, and I skipped down the hall to get ready for bed.

I HAD A HISTORY; THERAPY HELPED

I kissed a lot of toads before I met Tommy. Brought up as a Christian, I believed that God had the right man out there for me, and I desperately wanted to be in a relationship. While dating my commitment-phobic friend Danny, I'd meet someone else and think; maybe he was "the one." It wouldn't take long to figure out that the new guy was a loser, and I'd go back to seeing Danny, only to do the same thing all over again. The last breakup I'd had before meeting Tommy sent me into therapy. That one ended so abruptly, I cried in my beer and hardly ate for two weeks. I lost so much weight that my twelve-year-old son looked at me across the table wearing the saddest face I'd ever seen and said, "Mom, why won't you eat?"

That was when I knew I needed help. In those therapy sessions, I discovered that since all I knew as a child was dysfunction, I gravitated toward it. Deserted by my father, molested by a doctor at the age of four and again by my stepfather's brother when I was six, I had a lot of self-esteem issues, which made me an easy target for jerks and womanizers. Through therapy, I learned to appreciate myself and my accomplishments, turned my creep attracter off, and insisted on better treatment from interested parties.

* * *

There was no game playing with Tommy. That was how I knew he was different. We were inseparable from the start. We were happy and couldn't get enough of each other. After only three months of dating, Tommy officially moved in. He had been spending the night at my place since our first intimate evening together, so it made perfect sense. On a Monday after Tommy, Allen, and I enjoyed a fun weekend of playing darts, eating pizza, and generally enjoying each other's company, the timing seemed right to discuss it with Allen. Since Tommy was at our house all the time anyway, my son didn't see how his moving in would make any difference.

I knew the adjustment to sharing me would be hard for my little man-child, but he liked seeing his mama happy. I never felt so wanted and important to a man in my life, and it was a fantastic feeling. When you find someone who is crazy about you, it's not too hard to look past his flaws. It was easy to delude myself that Tommy's drinking habits were not a big deal or wouldn't become a problem.

We'd been living together for about two months when Tommy got laid off from work. When I heard the news, I freaked out. I knew if he didn't find work soon, it would be detrimental to our relationship. Men had taken advantage of me for years, and I was finished with that phase of my life. The day he came home and broke the news to me, I was beside myself.

"What happened? Why did they let you go?" I asked.

Tommy worked as a food machinery technician. When he explained that it was the nature of the industry to let people go and reshuffle divisions, he added," Don't worry, honey; I'll find work soon."

I prayed that he would, but two months later he was still unemployed. While Tommy was out of work my brother Jake, who lived in Seattle, came for a visit. They hit it off right away and became best buddies. What should have been a good thing did not work out that way. The boys played pool and drank all day while I was at work. I came home to find them drunk, yukking it up and talking about what a great time they had. Finally, one day I blew a gasket.

"So how many interviews did you go on? How many applications did you fill out?" I was screaming at Tommy.

"Your brother is only here for a couple of weeks, and I didn't want to leave him with nothing to do while I went out job hunting. Besides, I've filled out lots of applications. Nobody is hiring right now."

"I appreciate that you want to show my brother a good time, but you have to have priorities. Where the heck did you get the money to drink and play pool with?"

"I got my unemployment check."

"That's great. You certainly won't have any money left to help with the rent, will you?"

"I'll have some. Please quit yelling at me in front of Jake and Allen."

"Jake leaves in a couple of days, and then you'd better get real serious about finding a job," I said, and stormed down the hall.

* * *

One evening after work, I sat Tommy down. It was time for a heart-to-heart talk.

"Honey, I'm afraid you're going to have to move out until you get your life together," I said. "I love you and I want things to work out for us, but my feelings for you are dying because of this situation. If we keep going on like this, I'm afraid that I'll stop loving you."

After a few moments Tommy said, "If that's what you want, I'll call my old roommates and see if I can move back in with them."

"That's it? You're just going to move out? No, 'I'm sorry I haven't been trying as hard as I should'? No, 'I don't want to live without you, babe'?"

"I don't know what you want me to say. You just said I needed to move out. I thought I was giving you what you wanted."

I stood up. "Men are so stupid," I said with a grunt, and went to bed.

* * *

The following two months were brutal. Though I wanted to be with Tommy, I sent him some pretty mixed messages. The first time we spoke after he moved out, he reminded me that I told him he needed to leave but then made love to him and held him all night long. I got up that next morning and told him that he should be gone when I got home from work. I also continued to call him just to hear his voice and tell him how much I missed him. All I wanted was for him to get a job and stop drinking like a fish so that we could be together again. Whether it was the Venus-and-Mars thing or my poor communication skills, Tommy didn't understand it at first. The fact that I went back to dating Danny again didn't help matters, either. But my old boyfriend was just a distraction. I never stopped longing for Tommy.

While we were apart, Tommy wrote me beautiful letters affirming his love for me. He said he was praying for us daily and that he wanted to change *for us*. I read his letters and cried, and I also prayed that he would get a job and get his life together. I didn't want to lose him. I just wanted things to be right. I never loved a man the way I loved Tommy. It was almost three months later that Tommy found a good job at a very reputable company. He immediately felt better about himself, and I felt better about us. We quickly resumed our relationship. When he'd been at his new job for about a month, I asked him to move back in.

* * *

We were a couple again and I was ecstatic. I fixed dinner every night for the family and prepared Tommy's lunch for work every evening before going to bed. I was getting better at picking up after myself, and asked Allen to do the same. Tommy became the voice of authority. Allen was used to running over me and not listening, but surprisingly he listened to Tommy. My guys were getting along pretty well and we became a family. Compared to the dysfunctional household I grew up in, we were living like the Cleavers.

About five months after Tommy moved back in, I decided we should buy a house. I'd seen an infomercial for a product that claimed, "By using this kit you will own a house in six months, even if you don't have any money for a down payment." It sounded great to me, but Tommy thought I'd lost my marbles. By then he'd figured out that if I put my mind to something, I will get it done. I ordered the kit, and while the formulas suggested didn't work in California, it gave me a little know-how and the courage to go after the dream of owning our own home. Even though my savings weren't enough for a down payment, by the grace of God, five months later we moved into our first home in Hollister.

FAST, TUMULTUOUS, PAINFUL, WONDERFUL

HOLLISTER — OUR NEW HOME

"I can't believe you pulled it off, honey," Tommy said as we stood in the middle of our living room with stacks of boxes all around us.

"It wasn't easy, but we made it. We won't be going out to eat or buying any new clothes for a couple of years, but at least we have our own home. Allen is already out front making friends with the neighbors. Can you believe it? In San Jose we didn't even know our neighbors' names. It was so nice of Frank from next door to bring us a bottle of wine and those wonderful cookies. We'll have to invite them over for dinner when we get settled and on our feet."

"That won't be anytime soon, honey," Tommy said. "I'm glad we took our vacations for the move. There's no way I could drive back and forth to San Jose, work eight hours, and come home and unpack these boxes."

"Who are you kidding? You know who is going to wind up unpacking all of these boxes."

"Well, you're the one who knows exactly where everything belongs. God forbid I decide where to put anything."

"Honey, the garage is all yours to do with as you please."

"Thank you so much; *you're highness*."

Hollister — Our New Home

"Don't mention it. Now help me move the couch over by the sliding glass door."

* * *

For the next two and a half years Tommy and I both worked hard to get on our feet. Money was tight. We had to make the mortgage payment, put money toward the loan from my mother, who lent us the down payment, as well as make payments on a loan from the seller's Realtor to cover closing costs. Somehow we got through it. A night on the town was dinner at Round Table Pizza. Still, life was good.

* * *

Tommy proposed five months after we moved back in together, but we decided to buy our home first and then get married. Now that we had settled into our new house, it was time to make wedding plans. My roots in Christianity went deep, and I always wanted a church wedding. Tommy had been married two times, but neither of them in a church. He liked the idea of being married in God's house and thought it might improve our odds for success. I found a nice church and made an appointment with the pastor. We were both nervous. Neither of us had regarded spiritual issues for quite some time. Pastor Rodriguez was the deacon of the First Presbyterian Church. He was a very pleasant and unpretentious man.

"So you two want to get married," he said. "Tell me a little about yourselves."

"We have been together for almost four years," I said, jumping right in. "We have a house here in Hollister that we live in with my fourteen-year-old son. Tommy is divorced and has three children. They all live in northern California, but he's been estranged from them for a long time. We're hoping to improve that situation. I have been a Christian since I was nine, but I haven't gone to church regularly for quite some time. We are looking for a church home. We both know that we should be attending somewhere."

"Wow, did you have that summary written down somewhere, or did you memorize it?" the pastor asked.

"I wasn't sure what kind of questions you'd be asking, and I like to be prepared. It's important to me that you know we are Christians, despite the fact that we don't go to church."

"What church were you attending when you became a Christian, Charisse?" the pastor asked.

"I was brought up Baptist and then Pentecostal. I'd like to find a happy medium."

"What about you, Tommy? What is your religious affiliation?"

"I've gone to a variety of churches in my day, but the last church I attended was Jehovah's Witness."

"Really? Let me ask you: Do you believe in the Trinity—the Father, Son, and Holy Spirit?"

"I'm not sure what you mean. If you're asking whether I think God and Jesus are the same, no, I don't. Jesus is God's son. He can't be His son and God."

"Would you be open to sitting down with me to discuss the issue? We'd need to have some counseling sessions together before I could marry you. I wouldn't be able to perform the ceremony unless you're both Christians."

"If you're saying that you can't marry us unless I think Jesus and God are the same, then we have a problem."

"I'm sorry, Tom, but those are my convictions. You can find another pastor and still rent the church for your wedding. I can give you a couple of names."

Tommy was thrilled to have that option. We both thought the church was beautiful, and it had plenty of room for our hundred and fifty guests. We shook Pastor Rodriguez's hand and headed to the parking lot. The sun was shining, and the clean smell that a good rain leaves behind filled the air. It added to the feeling of expectancy.

As we got into the car, I asked Tommy, "So you really don't believe in the Trinity, honey? It's all I've ever been taught, so it's hard for me to grasp the idea that someone who believes in the Bible doesn't believe in the Trinity."

"No, I don't. Jesus is God's son; He is not God."

"But the Bible says that The Father, Son, and the Holy Spirit are one."

"Where does it say that? You show me. It doesn't make any sense. Jesus can't be God and God can't be Jesus."

"I know it's hard to understand, and I don't know exactly where to find it in the Bible, but here's how it was explained to me. Water becomes ice when frozen, right? And it becomes steam when boiled. But water is still water. The water symbolizes God, the steam equals the Holy Spirit, and the ice represents Jesus. They are all water, and yet they are also ice and steam."

"Thanks for the analogy, but it still doesn't make sense to me."

"I hope it does one day, honey. I believe that it's a pretty important facet of the Bible and a Christian life."

After debating the point, Tommy finally said, "I'm not a very good Christian, but I know I'm going to heaven. My God is a forgiving God. The Bible says if you believe in Jesus and believe that He is God's son, you will see heaven."

"Our philosophies may be different, but we do agree on the main point. Jesus is God's son, and without knowing Him, you don't get into heaven. It's clear He looks out for us even if we don't deserve it. Lord knows I haven't been an exemplary Christian, but He brought you and me together, so we must be doing something right. We have a lot to be thankful for."

"Yes, we do, but I'm not going to tell a preacher what he wants to hear so that we can get married, so I hope you can find someone else."

"I'm sure I will. I'm just thrilled that we're finally going to make it official. We'll be husband and wife."

"Mr. and Mrs. Horsfall," Tommy said.

His mention of the name triggered a new debating point. "I'm not real sure about that part, honey. I've established all of my credit in my name, and I don't want to start from scratch. You've got the back child support debt, too. I don't want to hurt your feelings, but I really want to keep my last name. Women do it all the time nowadays."

"Are you going to hyphenate it, at least?"

"Can you imagine me trying to write out Charisse Tyson-Horsfall every time I sign my name? You can't even say it fast three times. Just try it. Charisse Tyson-Horsfall. Charisse Horsfall is too hard to say. I'm sorry, but I really want to keep my name."

"Whatever."

"Oh, I hate it when you say that. You aren't going to be mad at me, are you?"

"I'm not mad. I'm disappointed."

"I love you."

"Don't try to schmooze me now."

We stopped by our local watering hole for a drink to toast our upcoming nuptials and played some shuffleboard and keno, and Tommy forgot all about the last-name debate. Allen was staying with a friend, so we had the house to ourselves and enjoyed a little romance.

AT LAST: MARRIED!

We were married on July 24, 1993. We found another pastor who married us at the First Presbyterian Church, and it was beautiful. Being a route driver in Hollister afforded me some great connections that saved us a bunch of money on our wedding. A customer hooked us up with the flowers for a really good price, and I borrowed my wedding dress from a coworker's wife. I was only going to wear it once, so it seemed silly to spend a bunch of money. For the cost of having it cleaned afterward, I had a gorgeous dress. It was white with a long train and had a V-neck with lots of lace. The silk sleeves were puffed at the shoulders and finished in a sheer lace design. When my mother saw me in it, she cried.

When the inexpensive hall we rented didn't pan out, we made the decision to hold the reception at our house. Thankfully, my pal Steve from my work and his wife, Vicky, helped us get our home ready for the reception. We cleaned, weeded, and planted flowers. We filled our backyard with rented tables, chairs, and umbrellas. Peach-colored decorations adorned all the tables and matched our wedding colors. It was absolutely beautiful. Our good friend and neighbor Boomer barbecued tri-tip and chicken in front of his house two doors away. Everyone living on our cul-de-sac was invited for the festivities. The deejay set up in our front doorway, and our driveway and court became the dance floor.

With the exception of one of the groomsmen locking himself in our garage when he went to the house from the church to get us ladies some champagne, and one of my bridesmaids rolling down our driveway after one too many beverages, the wedding and reception went off without a hitch. Many people told me it was the most fun wedding they had ever been to. Our life as Mr. and Mrs. was off to a wonderful start.

I was thirty-four when we got married. I loved referring to Tommy as my husband. For months after the wedding, I would say at every opportunity, "My husband" this, or, "My husband" that. I'd heard couples say that their relationship was great while they were living together but fell apart when they got married. Our love for each other had never been stronger. We were getting on our feet financially. I had secured a Hollister route at my company, which allowed me to pick up Allen from school and get home early enough to fix dinner. I had a man who loved me and accepted my son. Life was good. I thought it would remain that way forever.

TEENAGE REBELLION, JOB TURMOIL, AND PSYCHOTHERAPY

Sadly, our happy-go-lucky existence did not last for long. Like most teenagers, Allen thought he knew everything and his parents knew nothing. His insubordinate attitude and the way I handled it put a lot of pressure on our marriage. Tommy drank to evade the issues, and I moaned and grumbled constantly. Along with the stress of dealing with a rebellious teenager, there were rumors that my company was going to be sold. If not sold, it was going to close up shop completely. With a large mortgage payment hanging over our heads, I became terrified about our financial well-being. Though we were on our feet financially, we certainly hadn't been able to put money away for a rainy day.

Every day I went to work and heard a new rumor. The company's financial future was shaky at best. I'd been working at our favorite local tavern, The Office, on Saturdays for the extra money, but it certainly would not sustain us. I had no idea what we would do if my company closed. I had been at Granny Goose Foods for nine years by then. My store owners and bosses were happy with my work ethic. I did things right or I didn't do them at all; that personality trait attributed to my breakdown. We constantly ran out of product. I would have ten feet of space that needed to be filled and not enough product to fill the shelves. Making my shelf look good before I left a store became downright impossible. Store owners were complaining that customers were upset because they couldn't find their favorite items. The constant pressure to do things right, even when I didn't have the tools to do it, tore me apart. I was a perfectionist, when I couldn't do things the way I thought they should be done, I had a hard time accepting it.

At the same time, things with Allen were getting worse. He was mouthy and disrespectful. He didn't do anything that Tommy and I asked him to do. Tommy was a much better disciplinarian than I was, but I bucked him at every turn. As a child, I always felt like my mother's men were more important to her than her kids. I never wanted my son to feel that way. Consequently, I didn't back Tommy when I should have, which caused a lot of undue animosity between the two of them. Many times, I knew that what Tommy was saying was right, but when the words were delivered by a man who had been drinking all day, they lost validity.

I took Allen to a therapist to work on our family issues. Her name was Dr. Elizabeth Lee, and without her guidance, I might have lost my mind. She told me at our first meeting that she thought I was close to a mental breakdown, and that I needed to take care of myself before I could be of any help to anyone else. She was so concerned about my mental state that she offered me my first session for free. That's when you know you're in trouble. She sent me to a psychiatrist for medication. He suggested I take some time away from my job and continue my therapy sessions. I wrestled with guilt for leaving my boss in the lurch, but not having the extra pressures of the job helped my mental state. However, the situation with Allen just got worse.

Tommy told me many times that he thought Allen was using and selling marijuana. I refused to believe it. "Not my son," I told him repeatedly. I'd never done drugs, and I told Allen repeatedly to stay away from them. This is how denial looks. What I could not handle, I refused to see. When Tommy found drug paraphernalia

Teenage Rebellion, Job Turmoil, and Psychotherapy

in my fifteen-year-old son's room, there was no more denying the problem. We put him on restriction, and that was when he decided to live with his father. Even though it was one of the most difficult and painful things I'd ever done, I let him go. The day we drove him to his dad's house in Pleasant Hill, I thought the emotional distress might kill me. When we left him there, I sobbed all the way home. I could not be consoled, and once home, I threw myself on our bed and thought I would die of heartache. Tommy came to bed and wrapped his arms around me and held me until I cried myself to sleep.

I woke up the next morning, and even though I'd been sleeping for fourteen hours, I was still exhausted. I was so emotionally drained that I had a hard time pulling myself out of bed. I trudged down the hall and found Tommy in the kitchen. He wanted to make me breakfast, but the thought of food made me ill. Tommy suggested I call Allen and see how he was doing. When I did, Allen told me how worried he was about me. His concern made me feel even worse, and after we hung up, I cried even more. Tommy suggested that we get out of the house.

It turned out to be just what I needed. We went to the Office. We visited with our friends, had a few beverages, and played some pool. I started feeling a little more human and ended up telling everyone who would listen that I had just done the hardest thing I'd ever had to do. They were all very sympathetic and assured me that I was not a bad person. I drank entirely too much, and since I had not eaten much for two days, I got looped.

When Tommy suggested we leave and get something to eat, I had a craving for a McDonald's cheeseburger, fries, and a vanilla shake.

Tommy said, "Well, if that's what you want, that's what you'll get, honey."

We headed home with our dinner, and I polished off the fries before we got the car into the driveway. Getting pie-eyed brought back my appetite. After we ate, we sat in the hot tub together, and Tommy told me how sorry he was that I was hurting so badly. Then we got in bed and Tommy made slow, gentle love to me and kissed all of my blues away. God, I loved this man.

A YEAR OF FIRSTS

JOHNNY'S - OPPORTUNITY KNOCKS

The combination of not having the stress of Allen and Tommy fighting all the time and the relief of not going to work at a company that was falling apart improved my mind-set and made dealing with Tommy's drinking problem more bearable. Although I took the antianxiety medication the doctor prescribed, I didn't really attribute it to the improvement in my frame of mind. The label warned not to drink while taking it, but I ignored the instructions on weekends. My good friend had been taking the same drug and drinking for years. I figured I could, too.

I enjoyed my therapy sessions with Dr. Lee despite the fact that she brought up Tommy's drinking, a problem I was trying hard to ignore. She told me I wasn't facing reality about how his drinking was impacting our lives. What I wanted was for Tommy to get a handle on his problem. I didn't want to change our lifestyle. We had made good friends and I enjoyed partying with them on the weekends. I did not want to give that up. Irrational, yes, but that's the truth.

I'd worked hard most of my life and was finally getting a break. I took great care of our home, saw to it that the bills were paid, and was thoroughly enjoying being a housewife. However, whether intentional or unintentional, Tommy made me feel bad about not going to work. He'd come home and say, "What did you do today?" I'd take it personally and assume that he was giving me grief. It's possible that it was all in my head, but I heard an inflection in his voice that compounded the workaholic guilt I was already feeling.

I continued enjoying my Saturdays behind the bar at The Office. They were therapeutic for me. The male customers complimented me on my looks and my personality and made me feel good about myself. Tommy was never one for flattery. He had no problem telling me that he loved me, but he never paid me any compliments. The ego boost I got from working on Saturdays was something I needed.

The owner of the Office had decided to sell it. One day, half joking, I mentioned to a regular customer, Tom Ament, that maybe I ought to buy the place. Tom was one of my favorite customers. He was Hollister's local mortician and had the sense of humor that one must have to do that job in a small town. He was always joking and clowning around and never failed to walk in with a smile on his face.

"You don't want to buy this place, Charisse," he told me. "You need to buy Johnny's."

The bar was familiar. I'd worked there for about three months while the Office was being rebuilt. Johnny's had a spot open on Saturdays and I needed the money, so I'd worked there during the remodel and brought my customers from the Office there, too. I enjoyed working there. Johnny's was a rustic workingman's bar; and they served great food. Many of the bar's regulars had been going there for years.

Tom knew that the new owner was struggling and thought she might be interested in selling it.

"A gal I know bought it about a year ago and changed the name to It's Showtime." According to Tom, it was a bad idea. She tried turning it into a dinner house, but Johnny's had been a staple in this town for more than fifty years by then. "I don't think things are working out there for her. I'll bet you could get a real good deal on it. Why not check it out and talk to the owner, Danni?" Tom said.

"I might just do that," I said.

Later that day I told another customer about the conversation I had with Tom, and he agreed with everything Tom said.

"As a matter of fact, the owner is a friend of mine," said Nino. "I'll give you her home phone number. Tell her that I told you to call."

"Thanks. I'll give her a ring."

* * *

As I dialed Danni's number the next day, I thought, *What am I doing? How am I going to buy a bar? What do I say when she answers the phone? "Hey, my friends tell me you need to get out of the bar business and they think I should buy your place?"* I was pondering my dilemma when Danni picked up the receiver. I introduced myself and told her that two mutual friends suggested I give her a call. She was a little surprised but suggested that we meet the next day. We made an appointment for ten o'clock on Monday morning. I hung up the phone feeling very excited about our meeting and what the future might hold.

* * *

That morning, after our Sunday breakfast, Tommy and I went to the Office to watch football. We mentioned to some friends that we were considering buying Johnny's and they thought it was a great idea. I still didn't know how I would pull it off, but the prospect was exciting. I had plenty of experience running a bar and knew that I could do it. The finances were another story. I assumed Tommy would think the idea was crazy, but he surprised me by being very supportive.

"If anyone can do it, you can," he told me. "When you put your mind to something, you usually get it done; I knew that when you managed to get us into our house."

As the day wore on, everyone was talking about Johnny's. The more people talked about it, the more excited I got. I hadn't even seen Johnny's in more than a year, but I was starting to dream already.

Johnny's - Opportunity Knocks

I was too excited to sleep that night and was pacing in front of Johnny's when Danni arrived. She was a pleasant lady with a warm smile. She was my height, with short brunette hair and soft hazel eyes. She introduced me to her cook and her bartender, got me a cup of coffee, and we sat down at the bar. She was open and friendly, and before I knew it, she had given me a brief depiction of the last fifteen years of her life. She and her husband, Ron, owned Whiskey Creek, another bar just two blocks away, and ran it for more than ten years. Her husband was killed in a boating accident in Monterey. Ron was washed overboard in bad weather and his body was never found. After the loss of her husband, Danni sold Whiskey Creek to a local Hollister couple, Dave and Carol Rivers, and moved out of state.

But she missed Hollister and her friends. When she returned, she decided to try the bar business again. While Danni was living in Texas, Carol and Dave also bought Johnny's. Why they wanted to own two bars less than two blocks from each other, I have no idea, but Carol had gotten tired of running two places, and things weren't going that well, so she sold Johnny's to Danni.

The bar business had changed a lot since Danni had owned Whiskey Creek, and she found out that it wasn't what she wanted to do after all. She admitted that she hadn't been giving Johnny's her best efforts. In fact, it wasn't odd for her to close the bar early and take all of her customers to Whiskey Creek. Whether it was her connection to her husband at their old place of business or her lack of interest in her new one, she knew that it was time to move on. After chatting for quite some time, I thought I might be just the person to help her do it.

"I've been in the business since I was seventeen," I told her, "either as a cocktail waitress or bartender. I was managing the bar at the Attic Restaurant by the time I was nineteen, and I worked there for nine years. My first job was at Denny's serving food on the graveyard shift when I was just fifteen, so I'm real familiar with the trade."

Danni's face lit up. "It sounds like you would be perfect for this place."

"I don't have a lot of money," I told her. "I'm waiting on an inheritance that I could use for a down payment, but I don't know how I would come up with enough money to buy the place."

"If you can come up with a decent down payment, I will carry a loan for the balance. You can make monthly payments, with reasonable interest, of course. Then I'll have an income and you'll have the bar you've always dreamed of."

"It all sounds too easy. I'll talk to my husband and get back to you tomorrow."

I left the bar with my head spinning. Could I really buy this place and make it a success? Could I make enough money to pay our bills? Danni showed me her books and she was barely getting by, though she admitted that she wasn't putting much effort into it. After reviewing the books, I felt certain I could do better. When Tommy came home that night, I couldn't wait to share the news.

"I checked out Johnny's today. Honey, I really think I could make something of the place. I can use my inheritance money for a down payment, and Danni said she'd carry a loan for the balance for us. I've looked into it, and what she's asking for the place is fair. This could be the opportunity of a lifetime. I'll need to do more business than she's doing if we're going to get by, but I really think I can do it. The first thing I'm going to do is change the name back to Johnny's. An old bar with that much history has to have its original name."

"Slow down, you crazy redhead," Tommy said. "I thought you were just going to check it out. It sounds to me like you've already made up your mind. Are you sure we can do this financially?"

"Your job is secure and you're making pretty good money. We'll be getting your booze at wholesale prices, and that will help," I said with a chuckle. "With my inheritance I'll have enough money to give Danni a down payment and have a little left for working capital. I'm getting ahead of myself. I don't even know when my inheritance is coming, and she wants me to take over on January first."

"January first? Are you nuts? It's almost December now."

Johnny's - Opportunity Knocks

"I know it sounds crazy, but it feels so right. It's what I've always wanted. Granny Goose is going down the tubes, so returning to work there is out of the question. I need to find another job, so why not go to work for myself? It's a great little workingman's bar with lots of regulars and a restaurant. I met the cook. His name is Ralph, and he seems like a real nice guy. He's been in the business for years. He makes great homemade soups, and everyone loves his burgers. Right now he's cooking lunches, then he goes home and has to come back to cook dinner. I think dinners are a waste of time. She only serves six to ten a night. I'm going to serve breakfast and lunch. Then Ralph won't have to work split shifts. He'll be happier, and I think it makes more sense. My own place, honey; can you imagine?"

"I hope it works out, but I hate to see you get your hopes up," Tommy said, and cautioned me to keep my plans quiet until I was sure about my inheritance money.

"You're right, honey. I'll call Danni and tell her that if my money comes through, I'm in. If I don't get it in time, it just wasn't meant to be."

* * *

Danni had more confidence in everything working out than I did. I expressed my fears. I had never done payroll or any of the bookkeeping that went along with owning a business. She assured me that she would be there every step of the way, and promised to help me with payroll until I felt comfortable. She also promised to help me with quarterlies when the time came. Danni had a vested interest in my doing well. If I failed, she got the business back, and that was not something she wanted to see happen. She was helpful, genuine, and kind. I felt certain she wanted me to succeed.

Tommy and I kept things under our hats, but Danni did not. I told people that I hoped it was going to work out but that nothing was final. Danni told everyone that it was a done deal. The pressure was on. I was scared. If my inheritance didn't come through and I couldn't buy the bar, I would be humiliated. I believe God had a plan for me even then. I got my inheritance money the day before we were scheduled to close the deal.

CHARISSE TYSON: BAR OWNER

It was New Year's Eve, 1995. The bar was packed with people from all walks of life. Some were dressed to the nines in suits and gowns,

Charisse Tyson: Bar Owner

and others were in jeans. The long bar had sixteen stools, and every one of them was occupied. The restaurant's six tables were covered with cocktails, and people were standing everywhere. A festive air permeated the building. Good ol' rock and roll was playing on the stereo, and everyone was drinking and laughing. Danni introduced Tommy and me as the new owners, and it felt glorious.

The customers and friends in attendance were as excited as we were about our new beginning. At five minutes to midnight, the two televisions were tuned to Dick Clark's countdown in Times Square. Ten, nine, eight, seven, six, five, four, three, two, one— Happy New Year! I threw my arms around Tommy and kissed him. "What a wonderful New Year's Eve, honey. Tomorrow we'll own this place. Am I crazy? We have a house payment to make."

He laughed. "It's a little late to be thinking about that now, don't you think? Besides, you know you'll be great at this."

Everyone shook our hands and offered congratulations. I was on cloud nine. A new chapter of our lives had just begun. We were enjoying a nice New Year's kiss when Danni interrupted us with a tap on my shoulder.

"Here you are, kid; she's all yours," she said, and dropped the keys to the bar in my hand.

"What is this supposed to mean?" I asked.

"The place is yours and we're going home."

"What do you mean, you're going home? We take over tomorrow."

"It's after midnight, which means it's January 1, 1996."

"What about inventory? What about the money?"

"We'll worry about inventory tomorrow. I'm pulling my money out of the register, so whatever you make once I leave is yours to keep."

"What about change? I don't have enough money in my purse to break a twenty. Not to mention that I've been drinking all night. If I'd known you planned on walking off tonight, I would have slowed down hours ago."

"I'll leave the customers with plenty of change. Let the regulars run a tab and come back and pay you later. They're good for it. You look fine to me," she said, and with that, she and her daughter, who was tending bar, walked out the door.

I turned to Tommy. "This is insane. I think she may have shocked me sober."

He laughed again. "I hope so, because now you're in charge."

I'd been drinking beer and shots of Hot Damn all night, but I had no choice. I jumped behind the bar and started pouring. I had been helping Danni out by bartending for about three weeks by then, so I was familiar with the place. I poured like a fiend, and one thirty came fast.

"Man! I am thrilled to give last call," I told Tommy. "We've got to be back here in five hours, so let's just clean up the glassware and lock this puppy up."

"What do you mean, five hours?" Tommy grumbled.

"We've got a heck of a lot to do and only four days to do it. I've already placed an ad in the paper that says we're opening on the fifth. You can sleep in until seven thirty, honey, but I've got to have this whole place inventoried before Danni gets here."

We picked up all the glassware, dumped the garbage, and for the first time I locked the door to my bar. You couldn't have slapped the smile off of my face.

* * *

Full of anticipation, I was wide-awake at five thirty a.m. Even though I'd had less than four hours' sleep, I couldn't wait to get the bar ready to reopen. I threw on some sweatpants and an old T-shirt, kissed Tommy on the forehead, and took off for Johnny's.

As I turned the key to open the door, I knew it was meant to be. The pieces fell together perfectly. I'd spent nine years with a company that was now folding. My inheritance from my great-aunt came through just in the nick of time. This was destiny. When Danni showed up at nine thirty, the place was clean and the liquor and beer inventory done.

"You look pretty good for someone who was out late partying. How did the night go?" she asked.

"It went well, no thanks to you, you little shit. I can't believe you handed me the keys and walked out. I never saw that one coming. I certainly wouldn't have been downing the beers and shots if I'd known your plan."

Charisse Tyson: Bar Owner

"You were fine. I figured you might as well get broken in right." We laughed and then proceeded to go over the inventory together. When she left, I loaded the food from the refrigerators into ice chests to make room for the walk-in box we were having installed.

A wonderful group of friends pitched in on the remodel

Miracles and Grace in an Unlikely Place

Customers helped themselves to beer and left the money on the cash register while we worked.

Charisse Tyson: Bar Owner

Toasting our accomplishments with Our good friend Budman

Tommy and I worked like dogs for the next four days. He opened up the wall between the restaurant and bar to make it feel more spacious, painted the entire inside of the building, moved electrical wires, and installed new lighting in the bar area. My job was much easier than Tommy's, but when we were finished, I felt certain no one was going to recognize the place.

The day before our scheduled opening, we stayed until one o'clock in the morning putting the finishing touches on Johnny's. With six hours to opening, we still had half of the ceiling to paint. That was when Tommy put his foot down. He was exhausted.

"We can't keep this up," Tommy said. "It's time to go home."

"We can't open tomorrow in the morning when the place isn't finished being painted."

"I'm sorry, but sixteen hours of labor is enough. I'm exhausted and going home."

"I've been here longer than you, and I'm the one tending bar and serving food in the morning. Don't you understand that people are going to get their first impression of us tomorrow?"

"Then you should have given us more than four days to get this place ready. You're always in such a hurry. You want everything done right now. You made the decision to open so soon, not me. I'm going home. You should come home with me. Everyone knows we've been working our asses off, and nobody cares if it's not perfect except you. Put the roller in the sink and come home."

"You go on home. I'll try not to wake you when I come in," I said in a snappy tone.

When I finally did get home, every inch of my body hurt. The last four days had been long and grueling, but we had accomplished a lot. So many wonderful friends helped out. We already had a great clientele in place. My friend Stan had sold the Office, and many of the regulars whom I'd been waiting on there were looking forward to hanging out with us at Johnny's. As I crawled into bed next to Tommy, he told me how crazy I was and kissed me good night. When the alarm went off at five thirty a.m., I was painting in my sleep. I'd been in bed for only three hours, and I didn't know how I was going to make it.

"How will I get through this day? I'm so exhausted," I grumbled to Tommy as I reluctantly climbed out of bed.

"You're the one who couldn't leave until you painted the ceiling."

"That's because I like things done right."

As I stood in the shower and the hot water beat down on my sore body, I thought about the excitement of opening the bar for the first time. It was the fuel that kept me going. People had been hanging around in the dust of the remodel, buying beers, with no complaints. But this was our first official day, and I wanted it to be great. I opened the bar at seven a.m., and at seven thirty the guys we came to know as "the Militia" came in. They informed me that they met every morning Monday through Friday for coffee. Most of the men were over fifty-five. They knew a lot of Johnny's history, and I enjoyed listening to their stories. When they left, they gave me six dollars for their two and half pots of coffee, and a buck for my trouble. I went into the kitchen to see how Ralph was coming along.

Ralph had been cooking for Danni for about six months. He hated the double back and was thrilled that I opted for breakfast and lunch. He didn't drive a car, and riding to work on his bike twice a day would have been tough on a young man, much less a fifty-four-year-old. Ralph had been a serious drinker for a long time, and it had taken its toll. He was tall and slim, with thinning gray hair. He had a frail look about him. Thankfully, he had been sober for eight years. He'd spent most of his life in the restaurant business. He cooked in the army and opted for a career as a chef after he got out of the service. He was a damn good cook, too. His soups were wonderful. Every Friday we served Boston clam chowder, and his was fantastic.

I had most of the morning to get organized. Johnny's had never been open for breakfast, so outside of the Militia, I had very few customers, which ended up being a blessing in disguise. But by noon, it was as if a bus pulled up and dropped off fifty people. I was running around like a chicken with my head cut off when Tommy came in. The bar was full of people hungry for lunch. The tables were filling up fast. The phone rang off of the hook with to-go orders, and I was overwhelmed. I wanted everyone to get the best service possible, but I couldn't keep up with it all. I apologized left and right. Tommy had been washing glasses and cleaning up, but I finally had to ask him to take orders from some of the tables. My husband is not waiter material, and things got ugly pretty quickly. Ralph couldn't read his tickets. Tommy neglected to ask the customers what they wanted with their burgers and steaks, as well as how they wanted them cooked. None of us were prepared for the turnout. We ran out of burgers, green salad, macaroni salad, and clam chowder. The cook's job included washing dishes, except he was too busy, and we ran out of clean plates and silverware. Thank God one of the regular customers jumped in and washed dishes. By two thirty p.m. we had served sixty lunches. We all were wiped out, and Tommy was just about as cranky as a man can get.

"Don't you ever make me wait on tables again," he snapped. "Why didn't you have more help lined up? You know I'm not a waiter."

"Danni's been serving about twenty lunches a day. I didn't know this was going to happen. I assumed Ralph and I would be fine alone. That poor guy cooked his butt off, and he's in there doing dishes. I'm the one who's had ten hours' sleep in the last four days, and Nikki doesn't get here for two more hours."

"I'm sorry, honey. I know you're tired, but I'm lousy at waiting on tables, so please never ask me to do that again."

"I promise I won't. Do you want another Korbel?"

"You bet I do. I poured this one two hours ago and it's all watered down."

When Nikki walked through the door at three fifty I almost kissed her feet. A southern girl from Dallas, she had the accent to prove it. We just loved to hear her ask customers, "What can I git for you, darling'?" Nikki was slender and had beautiful brown eyes, and shoulder-length brown hair to match. She was one of the best multitaskers I'd ever seen. I'd watched her work at a Mexican restaurant as well as at the Office, and knew I needed her on my team. She made everyone feel at home and could take care of a roomful of people without neglecting anyone. She was the only employee I hired besides Ralph. Until I got the business up and running, I planned on working seven days a week with a minimal crew.

"It looks like you all had one heck of a day, girl," she said.

"Holy crap, Nikki, that's putting it mildly. I'm whipped. I can't believe we served sixty meals. Poor Ralph's got to be dying. He kept up real well, considering that they all came in a two-and-a-half-hour period."

I sat down at the bar to rest, and before I knew it the room began filling up again. Everyone shook our hands and told Tommy and me how thrilled they were for us. The happy-hour food that Ralph prepared was gone in ten minutes. Before I knew it, I was back behind the bar again helping Nikki keep up. She's one of the fastest bartenders I know, and even she was overwhelmed. Tommy stocked beer and washed glasses while Nikki and I poured drinks as fast as we could. Things finally calmed down at eight o'clock, and I flopped down on a bar stool. I was so exhausted, I felt like I'd just finished fifteen rounds of boxing.

"Nikki, I've just got to go home and get some sleep. Will you be all right?"

"Sure, honey. You just get on home and get yourself some shut-eye."

"You've got the keys. Call me if you need anything. Come on, Tommy; let's go home."

THE GRAND OPENING—ENTER JEANA

The first month went by in a whirlwind. The regular customers were wonderful and appreciative. We had great days and usually closed by nine p.m., with the exception of Friday and Saturday nights, when we stayed open until midnight. I worked seven days a week and sometimes fifteen hours a day, but I didn't mind at all. My business was growing daily and I loved it. I planned an official grand opening party for Saturday, February 17. Nikki was scheduled to come in at one p.m. so that I could get the free food out for our customers. I was crazy with excitement.

At ten a.m. the day of the grand opening, the phone rang. It was Nikki. She said she had an earache and suggested that I call Jeana, one of Danni's bartenders, who came highly recommended. We had a busy day ahead and I needed help badly. I was relieved when Jeana answered the phone.

"Hey, Jeana, this is Charisse Tyson, from Johnny's."

"Oh, hi, there. What's up?"

"I'm in quite a pinch. We're having our grand opening today and my bartender is sick. Danni told me you were a wonderful

The Grand Opening—Enter Jeana

bartender. Would you be interested in coming in around one o'clock? It should be a great shift, and I'll pay you cash."

"Let me see if I can get my girls squared away and I'll get back to you."

When Jeana called back an hour later and said she'd be in at one thirty, I just about did a backflip.

A lot of my family was in town for the auspicious occasion, and by noon, friends started coming in for our big party. When I told the regulars that Jeana was tending bar, they were thrilled, and assured me I would love her and her Boston accent.

Jeana came through the door and was everything customers said she was and more. She literally lit up the room with her smile. It took her a while to get to the bar, because everyone stopped her to get a hug. She got behind the bar and it was as if she'd never left.

"Okay," she said, "who needs a beeah?"

Jeana and an awesome group of regular customers.

Miracles and Grace in an Unlikely Place

With the bar under control, I headed into the kitchen to deal with the food. Our friend Boomer barbecued tri-tip, Ralph made a huge pot of chili, and we had green salad and garlic bread. Family pitched in to help serve and keep glasses and plates picked up. Jim Alarcon, one of the employees working at the business next door, had a deejay business on the side. We hired him and he played great music that kept everyone dancing. I was on cloud nine. Everyone ate, drank, danced, and laughed a lot. The party was a huge success, and by eight p.m. Tommy and I were tipsy and physically drained. I asked Jeana whether she minded closing by herself. Her old pals were going to hang out and make sure she was okay. We left her the key and headed home for a good night's sleep. Man, was I glad we didn't open until ten a.m. on Sundays.

SAINT PATRICK'S DAY, 1996

Jeana & our resident Joe Montana

Me cooking corned beef

Saint Patrick's Day, 1996

Tommy helping, kinda

Miracles and Grace in an Unlikely Place

Saint Patrick's Day was upon me before I knew it. Many of my older regulars had told me stories about Johnny's legendary parties, and I planned on bringing the bar back to its days of grandeur. John O'Brien, one of our very best customers, was Irish in every sense of the word. When John was Hollister's city attorney, he had the clout to get San Benito Street closed in front of the bar so that the patrons could have wheelbarrow and wheelchair races. One year they flew the Irish flag attached to a hot-air balloon above the bar. The balloon climbed so high into the clouds, they got in trouble with the FAA.

Tom Ament loved participating in pranks, so I assumed that the year they'd hung a coffin on the wall with Timothy O'Leary—their imaginary friend—in it, it was his idea. They stuffed O'Leary with newspapers and dressed him to the nines, and they had a full-blown Irish wake for him. I really wish I could have been around in those days.

John O'Brien informed us that he wasn't going to be in town for St. Pat's because he would be skiing. "Of all the nerve," I told him. I couldn't believe that he was going to miss our first St. Patrick's Day. Tommy thought we ought to fix his wagon, so he built a makeshift coffin and I blew up a picture of John and put it on a stuffed body and hung him up on the wall. It was sure to add some fun to the party.

Some of the regular customers told me not to get my hopes up too high for a big day, because the holiday fell on a Saturday. "St. Pat's just isn't the same when it falls on a weekend," they said. However, my excitement about our first Saint Patrick's Day celebration at Johnny's could not be squelched. I decorated the place with everything Irish. We had shamrocks, leprechauns, and Irish flags everywhere. We had green beer, green wine and green margaritas. I was dressed in green from head to toe, including my socks and underwear. I cooked fifty pounds of corned beef low and slow, with loads of garlic, onions, and spices. Then I added carrots, red potatoes, and cabbage to the pots. Jeana said, "That's just about the best boiled dinna I ever tasted." I was dialed and ready for a fantastic day.

At eleven thirty a.m. the phone rang. I couldn't believe it! Nikki called and said that she had another earache. By now I knew what

Saint Patrick's Day, 1996

that meant. I'd never seen her drink behind the bar in any of the places she worked, but I knew she liked to party. I'd had no idea the extent of her problem when I hired her. I was so angry. Jeana was working already, and now I had to ask her to come in early. There would be only two of us to take care of customers, and I had to get the food out as well. I knew Tommy could help out, as long as I didn't ask him to wait on tables and he didn't start drinking too early.

Jeana was great about coming in early, even when I told her I had no idea how late she would need to stay. Ralph had been warming up the corned beef and boiling the vegetables during the day while he cooked lunches. Thank God he offered to stay and help with the complimentary meal.

"You are a gem, Ralph," I told him. "I know we're going to be busy, so if you can help Tommy with the food, I can help Jeana keep the cocktails flowing. I'm going to kill Nikki. I can't believe she did this to me again."

"You know, I used to have a drinking problem," Ralph said. "But I always got my job done. I've taken a nap or two in the walk-in in my day, but I never missed work because of my drinking."

"I'm so glad that you quit, Ralph. Two boozers around here are plenty for this girl to handle. I'm afraid I'm going to have to let Nikki go. She always pulls this crap on monumental days. What the hell is up with that?"

"For some alcoholics, that's just how it is. The more pressure to perform, the more likely we are to get drunk," Ralph said.

"Thank God for Jeana; that's all that I can say."

By four o'clock the place was jammed. We had Irish music on the jukebox, and everyone was eating, drinking, and having a merry time. The free corned beef and cabbage was a huge hit, and everyone thanked us profusely for bringing back the tradition. By eight thirty Jeana and I had green fingers from food coloring; sore feet; and lots of tips in the tip jar. The beer cooler was almost empty, and we were out of Jameson and Bushmills. It was finally slow enough for me to sit down and let her take the bar alone. I'd started work at six a.m. and I was dog tired.

"You close up whenever you need to, Jeana," I said. "This tired bod needs to go home." I checked on the kitchen, and Tommy had cleaned it up to the best of his ability, given his lubricated state. It wasn't the way I wanted to leave it, but I was just too tired to care. I would finish it up in the morning. Once again Nikki let me down, and Jeana and I paid the price. I was going to have to fire her whether I liked it or not. Jeana was ready to take her shifts, and I couldn't ask for a better replacement.

TOUGH LOVE AIN'T EASY

I called Nikki on Monday. She wasn't supposed to be back at work until Wednesday. I asked Jeana to work Tuesday night so I could do the dreaded deed. I was sick at the thought of firing Nikki, but she left me no choice. I dialed her number with my heart in my throat. Immediately, she made excuses about being upset over her ex-husband and apologized profusely. I told her I wanted to talk and arranged for a meeting the next day.

What I found when I got to her house broke my heart. Nikki was on the floor; her emaciated body was limp as a rag doll and her hair was caked with vomit. I'd never seen someone so ravaged by alcohol. Luckily, I was able to reach her sponsor, and he came and arranged to get her into detox. The entire episode made Tommy's drinking problem seem like no big deal. I remember feeling glad that his trouble with alcohol wasn't that bad.

TOMMY PROBABLY SHOULDN'T TEND BAR

Jeana was a wonderful and reliable replacement. She took a lot of stress off of me, but I continued to work seven days a week. It had been almost three months and I hadn't taken one day off. Tommy kept insisting that I couldn't keep going at that pace. Things got tense between us. It seemed the harder I worked, the more Tommy drank.

"You've got to take a day off," he said. "You are killing yourself. How long do you intend to keep this up?"

"I'm fine. I'll know when it's time to take a day off."

"I'm not putting in as many hours as you, but between my job at Hobart and all the projects I'm doing at the bar, I'm exhausted. I don't know how much longer I can keep working like this."

"You're right. You aren't putting in as many hours as I am. If you would go home when you get finished with your projects instead of staying at the bar and drinking, you wouldn't be so tired."

"The owners need to visit with the customers. It's good for business."

"Whatever you say, honey."

Shortly after that conversation, Tommy decided to quit his job. The phone rang one Monday morning at one a.m. and scared us

Tommy Probably Shouldn't Tend Bar

both out of a dead sleep. Tommy had been with Hobart for five years and was regularly on call, but he never got calls in the middle of the night. It was the straw that broke the camel's back. He had to drive an hour to San Jose, spend ten minutes fixing a machine, drive another hour home, and turn around and make the drive all over again two hours later. He was miserable and cranky when he got home that night, and announced his intentions to quit his job and start his own handyman business.

The idea of his quitting a steady job scared me, and I tried to talk him out of it. "Honey, we're doing pretty well right now financially because I'm working so hard. I can't keep this pace up and don't know if I can pay all the bills without your income."

"You're doing great. You said you've doubled the business that Danni was doing so far."

I assured him that when we got everything done at the bar, he wouldn't have to work so hard. He disagreed. "We're never going to get everything done at the bar. Every time I turn around, you've got another list for me. I can't deal with this crap anymore. I hate this job. I'm done with it."

"I can't tell you what to do. I know you're miserable, but the thought of not having your income is pretty scary."

If I had pitched a big enough fit, Tommy would probably not have quit his job. I don't really know why I didn't. He gave notice the next day.

I had no idea what I had set myself up for. My letting him quit his job gave him a lot more time to drink. In no time at all, we were going through a case of Korbel brandy every other week. The vodka was harder to track, because he wasn't the only one drinking it. I continued working seven days a week, and on Mondays and Tuesdays I worked from six thirty a.m. to nine p.m.

Tommy hadn't been working for about two weeks when he said, "You know, honey, I could close for you a couple nights a week. I did a fair share of bartending in my day."

"Could you work without getting drunk? It would set a real bad example if you're drinking on the job. Remember I had to fire Nikki because of her drinking."

"I can have a few and still take care of business. It's pretty slow after six o'clock; I'm sure I can handle it."

"Okay. We'll try it tomorrow, but you can't be drinking all day if you're going to work."

"It's settled then. You can have some time to relax. When was the last time you watched some TV on the couch?"

"I can't even remember."

* * *

The following Monday at six p.m., Tommy took over. I gave him a kiss, slapped him on the butt, told him to be good, and I headed home. It felt strange going home without him. I had a hard time relaxing, but eventually I went to sleep watching television. I woke up when Tommy came through the door.

"How'd it go?" I said groggily.

"It was fine. We had a great time. I shook the guys for drinks and won four out of six times."

"You look like you had six drinks, and you smell like it, too. You're lucky you didn't get pulled over on the way home. Did you lock everything up?"

"Of course I locked the place up. Don't be a buzz kill. We had a great night. I'm whooped, so I'm going to bed."

I followed Tommy to bed and wondered what kind of shape I'd find the bar in the next morning. I was already picturing all the things I was sure he hadn't done right.

When I opened the bar the next morning, I found a laundry list of things that Tommy hadn't done to my expectations. Instead of being grateful for the extra downtime, I was mad. There was water in one of the sinks, and the straw and napkin holders were left on the bar. The beer and the liquor were not stocked, and the bar looked like it had been wiped down with a filthy towel. I huffed and puffed around the bar, griping out loud the whole time. By the time the Militia showed up for coffee at seven a.m., I had myself worked into a dander.

"How are you this morning?" one of the guys asked.

"I'd be better if I'd just worked the bar myself last night. I let Tommy close up, and apparently he had quite a good time. He left plenty of extra work for me this morning."

Tommy Probably Shouldn't Tend Bar

"Sorry I asked. You just do what you need to do and we'll get our own coffee," he said.

When Tommy showed up for breakfast at eight thirty, he got an earful.

"I knew I should have just closed up myself. I finished putting things in order and getting ready for the day, and I've been here for two hours."

"What the heck are you talking about?" Tommy asked.

"You didn't stock the beer, and the bar was filthy."

"I didn't leave the bar filthy. I forgot to stock the beer and it took you two hours to deal with that? I'm sorry. I've never closed the bar before."

"That's why I left a checklist for you. I knew you didn't know all the stuff I do to keep this place running smoothly. If I have to come behind you and do everything, what's the point of my taking a night off?"

"I was trying to help. I came in for breakfast, not a lecture. Maybe I should go somewhere else to eat."

"If you're going to help me, you need to know what has to be done before you leave. And you really need to cut back on the drinking when you're behind the bar."

"I'm the owner, and the guys expect me to drink with them."

"Whatever. What do you want for breakfast?"

* * *

Tommy worked that night and things were a little better. I paced instead of resting while he was working, and he came home tipsy, but not as bad as the night before.

"I really wish you wouldn't drink so much while you're working," I told him.

The second Monday night that I left him to work I was very uneasy. I hadn't worked out since I bought the bar, and concluded that if I walked back to Johnny's I could check on Tommy and get some exercise, kill two birds with one stone, if you will. It was dark and a little scary, so I walked at breakneck speed, and in less than a half hour I was at the bar, sweaty and out of breath. Tommy was behind the bar, shit-faced, and the three customers sitting at the bar were just as loaded.

I completely lost it. "What the hell is going on here?"

Tommy's face looked like he had seen a ghost. I guess the sight of a sweaty, raving redhead would scare anybody.

"Everybody out," I screamed. "We are closing right now. You all look like you've had enough."

I'd never seen the bar empty so quickly. The unwitting victims of my rage didn't even finish their drinks. I gave no thought as to how they were getting home. I just knew my husband wasn't driving.

"What is wrong with you?" he yelled. "How could you embarrass me like that? Everyone was having a great time and you come in here and scare the hell out of them and run them off. What kind of a business owner are you?"

"Don't talk to me about being a business owner. You're behind the bar supposedly working, and you're wasted. Some kind of a business owner you are."

"People got their drinks and they were having a great time until you showed up. Screw this shit. I'm out of here."

"You are not driving your truck home in that condition. I'll close up the bar and take you home."

"If you can walk down here, I can walk home. I'm outta here."

Tommy stormed off. I closed the bar quickly so I could catch up and give him a ride. He'd never exercised a day in his life, and I was sure the walk would do him in. I jumped into his truck and caught up to him about halfway home. I rolled down the window and yelled, "Honey, get in the truck."

"I said I'm walking home. If you think I'm going to ride with you so you can give me some more shit, you're crazy."

By then, I'd calmed down and felt sorry for him. "I won't say any more. Just get in the truck, please."

"Hell, no! Go home and leave me alone, damn it."

Now I was angry again. I screeched off, with my husband in the rearview mirror. *Of all the nerve,* I thought. *He's mad at me, but I'm not the one who got drunk behind the bar.* I parked the truck in the driveway and went straight to our bedroom. I got in bed and waited for Tommy to come through the front door. The door opened and closed, but my husband never came to bed. That night he slept on the couch.

No matter how mad I got at Tommy, I didn't like sleeping without him, and never slept well when he wasn't there. At five a.m. I couldn't stand it anymore. I tiptoed into the living room, squeezed my way onto the couch behind him, and nuzzled up to him. "I'm sorry I went crazy on you in front of customers," I whispered in his ear. "Why don't you come to bed and snuggle with me?"

"You really embarrassed me in front of those guys."

"I know. Everyone was wasted and I just saw red. My mouth was moving before I knew what I was saying. I won't do that again. We may need to come up with another plan for me to take some time off, though. Having you work behind the bar is probably not the best thing for our relationship."

"You should hire some more help anyway. If you get sick, we'll have one hell of a problem on our hands."

"I'll start looking right away. In the meantime, we won't put you behind the bar unless we absolutely have to."

"That's fine with me. Let's go to bed."

As much as I hated fighting with my husband, I really enjoyed making up.

THE BIKE BLESSING OF 1996

Finding more help was a priority, but I had very little time to invest in it. Before I knew it, the annual Top Hatters Bike Blessing was around the corner. Danni explained to me that every Palm Sunday the local motorcycle club met at Johnny's, rode to the Catholic church up the street to have their motorcycles blessed, and then rode out to Bolado Park for a barbecue. She said we could expect about forty or fifty riders to show up around nine thirty a.m., and at noon they would all leave to head to the church. It sounded easy enough. Since breakfast was new to Johnny's, I looked forward to the extra restaurant business. What we got was a lot more than Danni had suggested, and I learned a tough lesson that day: Never plan on having a party the night before the Bike Blessing.

The Bike Blessing of 1996

The Jagermiester party 1996. One we'll never forget

Miracles and Grace in an Unlikely Place

The Bike Blessing of 1996

* * *

I planned parties at every turn for any reason when I first bought the bar. The day before the Bike Blessing we had a Jägermeister party. Jägermeister is one of the nastiest-tasting forms of alcohol known to man, but is reputed to contain numerous herbs with medicinal qualities. What it will do is get you seriously drunk. The Jägermeister girls—little hotties dressed in skintight black dresses—brought all kinds of party favors.

There were small basketball hoops with matching Nerf balls, little hand clappers, tattoos, hats, and T-shirts. And what a party it was. We played a very physical game of basketball, resulting in a couple of minor injuries. We sang and danced and put fake tattoos on one another. A couple of bald men left the bar with tattoos on the tops of their heads.

By ten p.m. the only people left standing were quite wobbly. Jeana played her usual chauffeur self and gave some people a ride, but I shudder to I think of the ones who got away. Tommy and I fell into bed, and I didn't know about him but my head was spinning.

The alarm went off at six thirty a.m., and I felt like someone had taken a jackhammer to my skull. I pulled myself out of bed and looked in the mirror to make sure that my eyes weren't bleeding. I looked as bad as I felt.

"Oh, Lord, I'm such an idiot," I said out loud. "If you make this pounding stop, I swear I'll never do it again. Please help me get to work."

Tommy felt bad, too, but was much more experienced at dealing with hangovers. Just getting ready for work was a chore for me. The blow-dryer was too loud on high, and it took way too long to dry my hair on low. I burned my scalp with the curling iron, poked myself in the eye with my mascara brush, and jammed my funny bone on the sink before I was finally prepared to get out the door.

We got to Johnny's at seven thirty, and for the first hour I didn't know how I was going to get through the day. Our, weekend cook Teresa, didn't feel much better. Lesson number two: Don't let your cook party like a rock star when she has to be at work the next day.

At eight forty-five we heard the roar of motorcycles outside the front door, and by ten a.m. there were so many bikers in the bar we didn't know where to put them all. Fortunately, not many of them wanted breakfast, because Tommy and I had a rough time keeping the beers, Bloody Marys, and screwdrivers flowing. We ran over each other, almost knocking each other down many times. We snapped at each other and then apologized repeatedly. Teresa tried to pick up empty beer bottles, wash glasses, and get us ice, but she was green around the gills. At promptly twelve noon a whistle blew, and just as fast as the room filled up it emptied. The three of us dropped onto stools and laid our heads on the bar.

Danni's approximation of forty or fifty motorcyclists was actually more like two hundred. We did two days' business in three and half hours and decided to close up for the day and go home and get some much-needed rest. I didn't get any complaints from

The Bike Blessing of 1996

Tommy or Teresa. We locked up and went home to the couch, where we stayed until it was time to go to bed. I decided that I needed to try a little harder to find extra help.

* * *

A few days after my resolve to hire more help, a short gal with long, thick, curly hair slid onto a bar stool and ordered a Budweiser. It was the slower part of my morning, so we had plenty of time to talk. When I found out that she was looking for a job I was thrilled. She started working for me that week, and I took Saturdays off and gave them to Teresa so I had the day to catch up on book work. When I was finished with the books, Tommy and I hung out and enjoyed our customers. Darts became our Saturday thing, and our closest customers and friends never failed to join us. I was relieved to be working a little less and enjoying my customers more, and it eased the tension between Tommy and me as well. He was right: I needed some downtime. Despite giving up three of my shifts, I still never took a day away from the bar. I enjoyed watching people have a good time in my place, and was proud of the business I had established. Things were going well—and they were about to get even better.

KARAOKE: A TRADITION BEGINS

A group of our original karaoke singers.

Karaoke: A Tradition Begins

I was cleaning the salt and pepper shakers when Jim, my unofficial deejay, came in for breakfast. Jim was a quirky guy. He had a type A personality and was an energetic workaholic. He had been doing a karaoke show at the Office on Wednesday nights for about four months, and my friend Lys, who was now running the bar for her brother, told me that it was a huge success. Every Thursday, Jim and Lys came in and told me how great karaoke was the night before, and I was jealous. I wanted a night like that too, so when Jim offered to try it at Johnny's on Thursdays, I was thrilled. I told him I had no intention of singing, though.

* * *

In an effort to make our first karaoke a success, we recruited many of our regular customers to join us. The Office had twenty or thirty singers a night, and when I looked at our little gathering of friends I panicked.

"Don't worry," Jim told me. "It's early yet."

He started out by playing a couple of dance tunes, and the bar began filling up a little. At least, all the bar stools were full. Lys came in to see how I was doing and offered to sing the first song. I was amazed at what a good voice she had. The crowd was very gracious and gave her a wonderful round of applause.

Inspired by Lys, another regular customer decided to give it a try. She didn't sound that great, but everyone cheered like mad. Then three more people signed up for a song. After six people sang, Jim tossed one of his selection books down in front of Tommy and me.

"Pick something out, you guys. It looks bad if the owners don't participate."

"You turkey, we told you we weren't singing," I said.

"You'd better pick something out or I'll pick one out for you."

"I told you I don't even like talking in front of a crowd, and you want me to sing?"

"Have a shot of courage and give it a try. You're always listening to country music, and everyone says you look like Reba McEntire. Do you know any of her songs?"

"I know a few. Let me have a look at that book of yours." I picked out "Have I Got a Deal for You" and ordered a shot of Hot Damn with a beer back. "If I've got to do this, I'm not going to do it sober," I said.

I was amazed that some of our customers had such good voices. There were some who weren't very talented also, and I told Jim to be sure and put me up to sing after one of them. Jim called my name and I slammed down another shot. My hand was shaking as I took the microphone.

"Don't let me make an ass out of myself," I told him.

I didn't even get off of my bar stool. I sat staring at the television with the words on it so I wouldn't have to look at anybody looking at me. When my song was over I got a huge round of applause.

Maybe this karaoke thing isn't that bad after all, I thought to myself.

"You need to try it, honey," I told Tommy. "It's actually fun."

"It'll take a couple more shots of Korbel before I even think about it."

"So have a couple more," I said.

Tommy took my advice, thumbed through the songbook, chose "Brown Eyed Girl," and turned his request in to Jim. When Jim called his name, he retrieved the microphone and stood in the middle of the room. I'd heard my husband sing along with the radio, but I had no idea what a wonderful voice he had. He did a fantastic job on the song, and when he was finished the room erupted into enthusiastic applause, with people whistling and clapping.

That night a tradition was born that we carried on for many years. We always had to get tipsy to sing, so Tommy started taking a cab to the bar on Thursdays. We went to dinner at a restaurant two blocks away when Jeana relieved me from my shift behind the bar at five thirty, and then it was back to Johnny's to drink more liquid courage, followed by singing our hearts out with our friends. We helped Jeana close up and then she drove us home. The ride to our house was always an entertaining one.

* * *

Jeana's old station wagon was the source of some pretty good laughs. It didn't have a reverse gear, and the windshield wipers

Karaoke: A Tradition Begins

didn't work. Jeana went out of her way to try to park where no one could block her in, although it wasn't usually an issue at one thirty in the morning. I did say usually. One Thursday night after another great time at the bar we walked out front and there was Jeana's car across the street with a car parked in front of it. There were no other cars on San Benito Street as far as the eye could see, but the one guy who left his car was parked right in front of Jeana.

"You must be kidding me," she yelled, and Tommy and I broke out into hysterical fits of laughter.

"It's not funny," she said.

"Oh, yes, it is, Jeana Beana. I'm glad I went to the bathroom before we left or I would pee my pants right now," I roared.

"Don't worry, Jeana," Tommy said. "Just get in, start it up and put it in neutral, and we'll push you back far enough so that you can get around the car."

"It's a good thing it's not raining," I chimed in.

We were laughing so hard that we had trouble mustering the strength to push the car. When we were sure that Jeana had enough clearance, Tommy and I jumped in. Tommy tried unsuccessfully to keep the car's headliner from lying on top of his cowboy hat.

"Jeana, you need a new car," he said. "Is this your way of trying to get a raise?"

"Whateva works," she said in her wonderful Boston accent.

Thursdays were filled with fun, laughter, friends, and lots of alcohol. I should have left well enough alone, but that just wasn't my style.

* * *

Always wanting to be involved in the community, we decided to sponsor four bowling teams for the Thursday-night league at our local bowling alley. We rounded up our teams in short order and another tradition was added to Thursdays. When sixteen of us and our cheering sections hit the Hollister Bowling Alley, everyone knew we had arrived. As always, the Johnny's group was the fun one, and everyone wanted to hang out with us. While bowling three games we drank shots of Hot Damn, sometimes running the bar out of it, along with plenty of beer, and then brought the drunken lot back to Johnny's. By the time we hit the place everyone was in a singing frame of mind, and a good time was had by all.

* * *

Thursday business grew quickly, and before I knew it, my fun-filled Thursdays with friends turned into a ballbuster. I had no time for singing because I was too busy stocking for Jeana. Everyone enjoyed themselves, and we quickly became the Thursday-night hot spot. Other bars in town gave up and closed early on Thursdays, because there wasn't any point in competing with us. Fridays were a little rough on me, to say the least, so I finally scheduled a bartender to cover my morning shift, so I didn't have to be at work until ten or eleven for payroll and bookwork. Friday lunches evolved into a two-person job, so I helped out while nursing my hangover.

* * *

As business grew I knew that I'd made the right decision in buying Johnny's. It may sound strange, but I felt like God was blessing my efforts despite the fact that we weren't living like Christians. We drank entirely too much; we didn't go to church, much less tithe; and our language was atrocious. We loved God, were good to people, and held charity events to raise money for many local nonprofits, as well as individuals. We were quite content with our lives and, for the most part, each other.

OUR HISTORIC SIGNIFICANCE —PARADES AND RALLIES

Miracles and Grace in an Unlikely Place

THE WILD ONE PUT JOHNNY'S ON THE MAP

When I bought Johnny's in 1995 I had no clue as to its place in history. Sure, I knew that the picture behind my bar was from the Life Magazine story about something that happened in Hollister, and that it was taken in front of Johnny's, but its true significance eluded me. This was pre-Google days, and the only way to find out about Hollister history was to hear it from the locals.

Mark Maxwell, a motorcycle enthusiast and Hollister history buff, enlightened me one afternoon. His passion to honor Hollister's place in history was contagious. He informed me that Johnny's was revered in the biker community because it was the bar that bikers rode their motorcycles through on the Fourth of July weekend in 1947, and the one depicted in the 1953 movie *The Wild One*, with Marlon Brando. He told me the framed 1947 *Life* magazine picture on my wall of a drunk on a motorcycle with beer bottles piled around it was staged by the media. The stories journalists wrote about the weekend were so exaggerated that they put fear of bikers into the hearts of many. When producer Stanley

Kramer capitalized on the event with his movie *The Wild One*, the image of bikers was forever changed.

* * *

On Fourth of July weekend in 1947, the influx of four thousand bikers to a small town of about twenty-five hundred overwhelmed the businesses and especially the sheriff. The bikers blew off a lot of steam, drank a lot of beer, urinated on sidewalks—because there weren't enough bathrooms to accommodate the crowds—and generally wreaked havoc, but people who were here at the time attest to the fact that it wasn't anything like the papers made it out to be. People believed what they read, and the incident sealed Hollister's place in history forever.

The fiftieth anniversary of the event was sure to draw a large crowd. A group of motorcycle enthusiasts were trying to put together a rally to commemorate it. With surely thousands of bikers rolling into town to celebrate the occasion, they wanted to see the city prepared this time, unlike in 1947. A trial run was planned for 1996 in preparation for the fiftieth. It was going to be a great opportunity for the city, and local businesses and nonprofits, to make some money. It sounded fantastic. I wanted to help in any way that I could, so I assured Mark that I would be at the city council meeting when the group asked them to sanction an event and let them use city properties for the venue.

As Mark left he said, "Thanks for your time, Charisse, and by the way, you are doing a great job with the bar."

"Thank you, Mark; I'm really enjoying it. The customers are wonderful, and we've made a lot of great new friends. Thanks for stopping by."

* * *

I couldn't wait for Tommy to come in so I could tell him about the bar's history. I found the whole thing so exciting. As soon as he came through the door I practically jumped him. When I told him what I'd learned he looked at me as though I were daft, shocked

The Wild One Put Johnny's on the Map

that I didn't already know all about Johnny's history. I'd been so busy running the bar that I didn't take the time to learn about its past. We were both excited and worried about what a motorcycle rally would mean for our business, and we attended the city council meetings that moved the agenda forward.

What we didn't know was that we would be embroiled in a never-ending battle with the city to have and keep a rally that brought thousands of attendees with money to spend in our bedroom community. Who would believe that city representatives wouldn't see its value?

1996 OUR FIRST RODEO PARADE

1996 Our First Rodeo Parade

Clampers were always a part of our Rodeo Parade

Johnny's location smack-dab in the middle of our main street has many benefits. Any parade that goes through town passes right by Johnny's, including the Rodeo Parade held late in the month of June. Hollister is truly cowboy country, and our annual rodeo and the preceding parade are big business for the town.

All of my firsts at the bar supplied lessons that I took with me from one year to the next. The Rodeo Parade evening was no exception.

Ray Wood, a Hollister police officer whom we came to know and respect, regularly stopped in at Johnny's in the evenings to see how things were going, and always took time to visit with Tommy and me and the customers. He was one of the nicest cops I'd ever met. The day of the parade, he stopped by the bar to inform me of what I could expect for the evening. He told me that during the parade people were allowed to take their drinks outside, but in exchange for the privilege, when the police said it was time to close, we needed to do so immediately. When he told me that it would probably happen around nine thirty, my mouth hit the floor. I couldn't imagine closing that early, but he assured me that I would see what he meant.

* * *

On my way to work at six thirty that morning I'd noticed chairs in front of some of the houses on San Benito Street. We had a really busy lunch, and when I stepped outside at three thirty to look around, folding chairs were lined up in front of every business as far as I could see. I'd lived in Hollister for six years and had never seen the parade. It was starting to look like it was a pretty big deal. The bar already had a good feel to it. There was a buzz in the air, and I knew that it would be a great night. By five o'clock there wasn't a seat left in the place. Jeana and I were both working hard, and the parade was still an hour away. We had our heads buried in the ice for four solid hours. Tommy stocked beer for us, and as soon as he'd put in a case of Coors Light it was time to bring out another one. I was out of regular Coors by six thirty, and Jack Daniel's was going like hotcakes, as well as Crown Royal. I was afraid that I was going to run out of everything before last call, unless it came at nine thirty, as Ray predicted.

The cowboys got louder and louder and rowdier and rowdier, and at nine twenty-five there was a loud crash as one of them was thrown right through my storeroom door. I was horrified. We had a pile of cowboys tossing one another around in my hallway, and I was screaming at the top of my lungs, "Stop it, you bastards. Knock it off and get the hell out of my bar." It took only minutes, and there was Ray and about five of his fellow officers pulling the cowboys off of one another. Ray looked at me and motioned a karate chop at his neck with his hand that said, *That's it; you're done.* I couldn't believe it. He'd called that within five minutes.

"I'll be damned if I'm gonna let these cowboys do this to me again next year," I vowed.

WHAT REALLY HAPPENED IN HOLLISTER IN 1947?

This picture, taken July Fourth weekend in 1947, was supplied by the San Benito County Historical Society. Johnny's was called The New Deal at the time. The building on the left with the neon sign is the bar.

Miracles and Grace in an Unlikely Place

Of the many accounts I've heard of the 1947 Hollister riots, the best explanation as to why things got so out of hand was given to me by Jack Jordan, a Boozefighter friend of mine who was a member of the Sharks Motorcycle Club at the time. He explained that many post–World War II vets had taken up motorcycling mainly because they couldn't afford cars. Without jobs to keep them busy, tinkering with their bikes and making them as fast as possible became a favorite pastime. They raced them often and were looking forward to the Hollister Gypsy Tour event. The American Motorcycle Association, which had taken over the tours in 1924, refused to let the vets race in Hollister, because they were not AMA members, and that was where the trouble started. The bikers decided to hold their own races on San Benito Street and took over Fifth and Sixth streets for their festivities. Johnny's location smack-dab in the middle made it the prime spot for watching the races.

An original Boozefighter, Kokomo on San Benito Street in 1947

What Really Happened in Hollister In 1947?

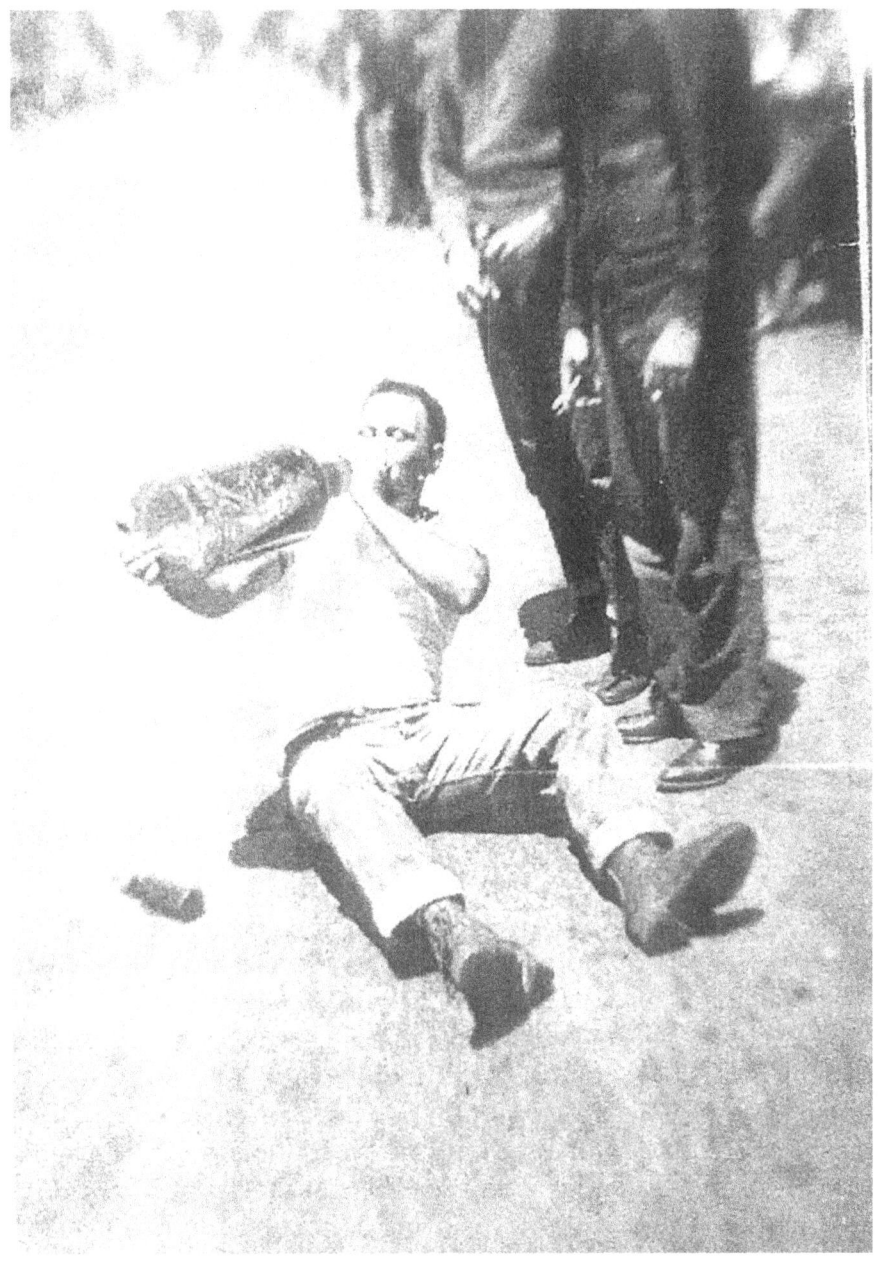

Wino Willie on San Benito Street during 1947 fracas

Miracles and Grace in an Unlikely Place

The Boozefighter Motorcycle Club, which was formed a year earlier in southern California by "Wino" Willie Folkner, had a huge presence in Hollister. They made Johnny's their official headquarters early into the weekend. It may have been because by Friday afternoon the bikers had consumed every beer in the county, and Johnny Matalitch, the bar's owner at that time, was the first to procure more. He was also a very gracious host and took the keys from a drunken rider and had him park his motorcycle in the bar to sober up before he would return them. The connection between the Boozefighters and Johnny's Bar & Grill was forever sealed.

I took this picture of Wino's plack at the site of the Mount Solidad Cross in Pacific Beach California. My Boozefighter friend Snowman grascuoisly took me there while I was visiting him in San Diego.

Wino was hired by the production company that made the movie *The Wild One* as a consultant. Lee Marvin's character, Chino, was based on him. Not very long into production Willie saw the inaccurate and malicious slant the movie was taking toward bikers, and he walked away without receiving a dime for months of effort. Wino was a beer-guzzling biker, but he had his standards.

THE INCEPTION OF OUR RALLY

In January 1995, one of Hollister's local newspapers, the *Pinnacle*, reported that Hollister city officials and the Hollister Downtown Association proposed the idea of using the fiftieth anniversary of the infamous Gypsy Tour as a moneymaking festival to help boost city finances. At that time, they were convinced a motorcycle rally would stimulate the city's economy. City staff passed memos among themselves emphasizing their leadership role in marketing and promoting the event.

Just one year later, shortly before the 1996 dry run, Hollister officials began backpedaling at breakneck speed because of criticism from law enforcement. Suddenly, city officials and the Hollister Downtown Association said that they were only working to get information to law enforcement, and that they had contacted promoters just to find out what the impact would be on the city. In complete contradiction to earlier memos, the acting city manager said, "The city has never sponsored nor intended to advocate for any event." The former city manager was blamed for promoting the idea that the city was actively planning and promoting a motorcycle event, and, as the city council's scapegoat, he was forced to resign. And so began the shenanigans and blame games of spineless Hollister city officials that would haunt and eventually kill our motorcycle rally.

THE DRY RUN RALLY OF 1996

Between the on-again, off-again plans for events in the county and the numerous rumors as to how many people would show up in Hollister on July Fourth weekend of 1996, planning for the event was nearly impossible. I was flying by the seat of my pants. I stocked up as best as I could, brought in family for extra help, and prayed that all would go well. Storage was quite a problem. Fortunately, Budweiser rented us a cold-storage trailer that held hundreds of cases of beer. My tiny little walk-in cooler could not fulfill our needs. Preparing for a weekend with an estimated attendance of two to six thousand bikers my first year in business was daunting. We rented a U-Haul truck for extra storage, and Porta Pottis for the parking lot—which has since become our patio—and enlisted the help of relatives and friends.

    I'd like to tell you that I have a clear memory of everything that happened that 1996 Fourth of July weekend, but that would be a lie. We'd owned the bar for only six months, and I hate to confess that at the time, I was so busy running the bar that the significance of having Wino Willie sitting at my bar with members of the Boozefighter motorcycle club that he started fifty years earlier went right over my head. Luckily, Tommy spent some time talking to Wino and introduced us. I was absorbed in taking care of business and didn't even stop to take a picture with him. I kick myself in the butt for that one to this day. Jeana was smart enough to take a picture of Willie, his son Clyde, and Huck; a local Boozefighter who came to be a wonderful friend. If it weren't for her I wouldn't even have a picture of a legend sitting on one of my bar stools. But I digress.

My one and only photo of Wino Willie taken at Johnny's in 1996.

On Wednesday, July 1, bikers started rolling into town. The Boozefighters showed up in droves. Wino hadn't been back to Hollister for forty years, and because of his presence, thousands of Boozefighters were in attendance. We were busy from the time we opened the doors at seven a.m. until we closed them at one o'clock in the morning. Our few employees, my family, and some regular customers all worked our tails off.

The Dry Run Rally of 1996

The bikers were the most gracious people I had ever met. Any fear I had about being invaded by bikers evaporated as I witnessed the respect they gave one another, me, and my employees. But by the time Sunday rolled around our tiny little crew was ready to see the bikers leave—not because we didn't enjoy them, but because we were so exhausted we could hardly stand up. So went the 1996 "pre-rally" and the only time I would get to see Wino Willie, because he died just days before the 1997 fiftieth-anniversary rally.

LIGHTS ON PARADE—A FLOAT, ARE YOU CRAZY?

Putting on the final touches while parked on Petaluma Court.

Lights on Parade—A Float, Are You Crazy?

I felt like the queen of the Rosebowl parade as we passed by Johnny's

Miracles and Grace in an Unlikely Place

Our first year at Johnny's was a whirlwind. The pre-rally led to Halloween, which led right into Thanksgiving, followed directly by the annual Lights on Parade, an event sponsored by our local downtown association. Every year on the Saturday following Thanksgiving, a parade of floats made by local businesses and nonprofits makes its way down San Benito Street. As with the Rodeo Parade, people line the streets with chairs early in the day so that they will have a good view of the festivities. As a new business owner in Hollister, I resolved to take part in all of its events. Because of my competitive nature, I was determined that not only would we build a float, but that our float would win best in show. I informed my husband that it was something we just had to do, and despite his vehemently disagreeing with me, a plan was hatched to build a float.

Many of our wonderful customers offered to help, but before I could concentrate on the project I had to get through the busiest karaoke night we'd ever seen. The Wednesday night before Thanksgiving was off the hook. The place rocked until two a.m., and then I had to return to Johnny's early to cook a full-blown Thanksgiving meal for our friends who didn't have a place to go. About twenty-six members of the Johnny's family were in attendance, and we had a wonderful time. Tommy said the blessing and thanked God for all of our wonderful customers and friends, as well as a prospering business. Then everyone ate, drank, sang songs, and played games. I was exhausted, but happy to bring so much joy to a great bunch of people. Sadly the workaholic spent most of her time in the kitchen and missed out on the camaraderie. I hadn't come to grips with my overachiever self, who missed out on most of the fun in order to take care of business.

* * *

The following Friday I offered up free pizza and beer for our helpers, and the building of the float commenced. One of our customers had a trucking company and not only offered to supply the twenty-five-foot flatbed that would house our float, but he also volunteered to pull it in the parade. Another friend Dave let us use his Harley-Davidson and volunteered to wear his Santa suit on the float. A wonderful artist friend painted the sleigh, and it was so gorgeous that it looked like it was right out of a Christmas storybook.

We turned the float building project into one heck of a party. When it got dark Tommy rigged some lights and we worked until eleven o'clock at night. It was frosty, but people just put on gloves and jackets and continued to work. We put planks in place and rolled Dave's orange Harley-Davidson up onto the trailer and decorated it with lights, and used tinsel as reins between it and the sleigh that Tommy built. We decorated the Christmas tree and put beautifully wrapped presents underneath it. We positioned a light-up snowman on a platform that Tommy built and surrounded it with lights. It was absolutely breathtaking. When we were finished we all stood back and admired our handiwork in silence. We were too awestruck to speak. I finally raised my beer and offered a toast. "To the best friends anyone could hope to ask for. We couldn't have done it without you."

* * *

The night of the parade the bar was so packed that I almost skipped riding on the float to stay and help the girls at the bar. I would have missed out on a wonderful experience. Tommy and I sat in the sleigh, and Jeana's daughters sat on the Harley-Davidson, with Dave in his Santa suit keeping watch over them. As we passed in front of the bar, the crowd went wild, and I felt like I was queen of the Rose Bowl Parade. I get goose bumps today remembering it. I got my wish: We won best in show. When I announced to the bar that we were the victors, they all but raised the roof with their cheers. To me it made all the stress and bickering worth it. Tommy may have a different opinion.

* * *

Christmas dinner with friends.

As with Thanksgiving, I cooked a huge meal on Christmas Day for customers who didn't have family plans, and once again about twenty people gathered around the tables that we shoved together so that we could eat family-style. As usual, Tommy said grace and thanked God for all of the wonderful people who made Johnny's feel more like a home than a bar.

Lights on Parade—A Float, Are You Crazy?

Decked out for New Year's Eve.

Miracles and Grace in an Unlikely Place

With Christmas behind us, I made preparations for the final holiday of the year. I planned a New Year's Eve dinner that included prime rib, filet mignon, lobster, and swordfish, and all our regular customers made reservations. I ordered tons of party favors and hired a band, and the evening was a huge success. Once I made sure that everyone had a glass of champagne and that all of the televisions were tuned in to the Dick Clark countdown, I joined my husband on the dance floor. He looked gorgeous in his tuxedo, and when he wrapped his arms around me I felt like the luckiest woman in the world. I reflected on how great Johnny's had been to us, and how blessed we were. There had been some hurdles, and Tommy and I had our issues, but I was truly happy. As I'd thought when I turned the key for the first time to my bar, it was meant to be. I looked forward to many years as owner of the wonderful historic place.

* * *

Planning events to keep the bar busy was my way of building up the business. I relentlessly came up with reasons to have a party and invite friends. I had birthday parties for all of my employees as well as regular customers. I even had a post-vasectomy party for my husband. The poor man sat at the end of the bar with an ice pack on his lap while the rest of us toasted his accomplishment and partied on. I made cocktail wieners and meatballs, and a really good customer made Tommy a cake that looked like a penis with a hatchet in the end of it. During karaoke the next night I dialed the house and the entire bar sang "Great Balls of Fire" to Tommy over the phone. Nothing was sacred in our group, and anything could be turned into a celebration. I think it's why people loved hanging out with us.

BUSINESS BOOMING AND I'M LEARNING

RODEO PARADE, JUNE 1997

Another Rodeo Parade quickly followed, and this time when Ray Wood came by I told him that I had extra help at the door and that I was going to see to it that I wasn't closed at nine thirty. He said that he admired my determination and wished me luck. I made sure that I had two bartenders on duty, as well as a bar back, so that I could be out on the floor keeping an eye on things.

The place was even more packed than the year before, and walking from one end of the bar to the other took me a full twenty minutes. I checked out everyone's faces, and anybody who looked like they had an attitude got an earful. It didn't matter how big a man was, I told him that he could lose the attitude and respect my establishment or get the hell out. I placed myself in between six-foot-plus cowboys, put my finger right up in their faces, and said, "Not here, boys. You will not get me shut down tonight. Lighten up or there's the door." Then I instructed the culprits to move to opposite sides of the room.

Things were going pretty well. I was feeling hopeful and proud when I noticed that it was almost eleven and we were still open. Putting a stop to the many arguments that could have turned into

Rodeo Parade, June 1997

fights had been a full-time and exhausting job. I was feeling pretty pleased with myself when I noticed an altercation breaking out near the ladies' room. There were at least five men involved, and I don't even remember how I made my way across the room as fast as I did, but I tried to drive my body right in between the idiots, all the while screaming, "Not in my house, you assholes! Knock it off, you sons of bitches." I got to the fracas before my bouncers. Jeannie, who worked for me and became my best friend, was behind me pulling me by the back of my belt and screaming, "Get out of there, Charisse. Get back here." My bouncers were pulling the guys apart when Ray and his men showed up. He gave me a look that said, *You know what this means,* and we were forced to close.

The crew sat around after we got the bar cleaned up and talked about the wild evening. Jeannie scolded me severely for getting in the middle of the brawl.

"You crazy nut, Charisse," she said. "Do you have any idea what could have happened to you? You could really have been hurt. Don't you ever do anything like that again."

"I didn't even think about it, Jeannie. I was there before I knew it. I just wanted those idiots to stop so we wouldn't have to close."

"And you thought one little redhead was going to stop six huge men from fighting? I'm mad, Charisse; I mean it. You could have been punched in the face or who knows what else. Don't do it again. Do you hear me?"

"Okay, pal, I got it. Well, at least we made it until eleven. That's an hour and half better than last year."

"We kicked butt, too," Jeana said. "All in all, it was a great night."

"Yes, it was. Imagine the Fourth of July weekend, ladies. We'll have four nights in a row like this, not to mention what the days will be like. I sure hope all of the extra help I've hired comes through. I think we're in for one hell of ride."

JULY 1997: THE FIFTIETH ANNIVERSARY MOTORCYCLE RALLY

Photo towers made it possible to take great shots of the bikes on San Benito Street

July 1997: The Fiftieth Anniversary Motorcycle Rally

A family member took this picture while standing in the middle of San Benito Street in front of Johnny's

Miracles and Grace in an Unlikely Place

A wise guy got up early to make sure he had a spot for his bicycle.

*A shot taken from across the street.
The city hadn't put the kibosh on our neon yet.*

July 1997: The Fiftieth Anniversary Motorcycle Rally

We took a picture of the aftermath on Sunday from Johnny's rooftop

There had been a lot of talk about how many people might show up in Hollister for the 1997 Hollister Independence Rally, and estimates were as high as a hundred and twenty thousand. A dedicated group of volunteers called the Hollister Independence Rally Committee had finally secured the go-ahead from the city council to put on an event. A stipulation that it wasn't the city's event or responsibility was included in the language of the contract. The HIRC worked hard to see to it that the motorcycle enthusiasts and bike club members who were predicted to show up in Hollister from every corner of the globe would have plenty of biker-related things to do, see, and buy.

San Benito Street was designated for motorcycle parking only from Fourth Street to South Street. It was estimated that five thousand motorcycles could be parked in the five-block distance, using both sides of the street and parking two rows of bikes down the middle. Photo towers were put in place at each end so spectators could get great shots of the spectacle. The side streets were designated for vendors, with two beer gardens, as well as two stages for musical performances and, of course, the Miss Hollister Independence Rally contest. There were bike contests planned, like the slow ride, the weenie bite, and the obstacle course, as well as a best-in-show contest for motorcycles old and new. As seemed fitting, Johnny's sponsored the vintage category.

The excitement in the air was contagious. Television and radio stations as well as numerous newspaper reporters called the bar for interviews. I was thrilled to have the publicity, but doing interviews while trying to prepare my bar for the crazy weekend was overwhelming.

* * *

With the enthusiasm I'd seen for the 1996 trial-run rally, and all the hype building up for the fiftieth, I knew I was in for a wild weekend. Plans were in place for the Return of the Wild Ones, a trade fair south of the Hollister airport. Return to the Gypsy Tour—an event that included races and a hill climb above Bolado Park—was organized, as well as the five-block party and fair on San Benito Street. Weekend at the Ranch, a campout featuring live music northeast of Highway 25, had its permit pulled shortly before the event by Sheriff Nyland because they couldn't pony up $143,000 for overtime for officers to patrol their two-hundred-and-fifty-acre site. The permit was reissued on appeal because the loss of hundreds of campsites would have increased the problems of housing a hundred thousand visitors to Hollister. As would always be the case, the city and law enforcement went out of their way to make things difficult for anyone making an effort to bring business into town.

It promised to be a great weekend, and people were either excited or scared and leaving town. Someone actually called and asked whether I wanted to rent them the bar for $20,000 for the weekend and take a holiday. Yeah, right, like that was ever going to happen. News crews from LA to San Francisco showed up wanting an interview, and I had to decline many of them because I was spread way too thin. If I could have cloned myself into four people

July 1997: The Fiftieth Anniversary Motorcycle Rally

there still would not have been enough of me to go around. I couldn't sleep for weeks leading up to the event, because I was constantly planning and wondering what I might have missed, even in my dreams.

* * *

It is almost impossible to describe the kind of preparation needed for an event that made it possible for us to do two months' business in five days. In 1997, besides myself, I only had three employees, so I needed to hire plenty of outside help. Once again, I had my family lined up to assist me, but I still had quite a few holes in my schedule. I met bartenders in the months preceding the rally who said they would love to work, and a friend I worked with at the Office volunteered. I tried to choose people I could trust. As it turned out, I wasn't a very good judge of character, or I just had a lousy pool to draw from.

People always assume that Johnny's is bigger than it is. Before we added the patio in 1999, we had only 1,250 square feet to do business in, and that included the kitchen and two bathrooms. In an effort to make it easier for people to get a beer, I added a small station for draft beer on the restaurant side of my building. My Budweiser distributor rented me a trailer again, and this time we put as much in it as it could hold and scheduled daily deliveries. I arranged for two extra garbage pickups and ice deliveries at least twice daily, and hired a security company for help at my doors. Tommy built a new storage and office area above the bar, and I stocked it with booze, cups, juice, food products, and T-shirts. I could hardly move or get to my desk. I bought loads of extra change and locked it in my safe. I thought I had it all handled, but, man, was I wrong.

* * *

On Tuesday, July 1, tents popped up on private property all over downtown, and vendors started rolling in. Many of them started their "setup workday" at Johnny's for breakfast. When they were finished for the day they came back to the bar to unwind, and they really knew how to let their hair down. We no longer closed at nine o'clock, and my girls put in ten-hour shifts, not getting out of the bar until one o'clock in the morning. By Wednesday, Boozefighters and Hells Angels started rolling in. Bob Valenzuela stated in his column in our local paper that the safest place to be in America was Johnny's, because the Hells Angels had claimed my place as their official headquarters. As soon as we opened the doors at seven a.m., the place started filling up. I didn't have half the help that I needed. I could never have dreamed of doing as much business as I was doing. By nine a.m. on Thursday, July third, I could hardly walk through the bar, and by Friday we had to start a line at the door at ten thirty in the morning, because I couldn't squeeze another body into the building. As with the Rodeo Parade and Lights on Parade, people were allowed to take their drinks outside, so even though I was full to the brim, new faces needed beverages at all times.

At this point in time, a law was in place that kept me from letting people under twenty-one in my building, because I allowed smoking. Alcoholic Beverage Control officers and the local police department came by and warned me that they would be looking for underage people in the bar. In my conversations with the head of the security company I hired, I stressed very strongly that my license was at stake. I told him to be sure that his men were doing their jobs and carding everyone to make sure that no one under the age of twenty-one came into my building.

I've come so far from the person I was back then that I hate to admit to being the raving lunatic that I was. But that's what I was, Hitler and the Tasmanian devil combined. It was my way or the highway, and you'd better not think about crossing me. I remember my brother approaching me with trepidation to inform me of an issue.

"Sister," Johnny said, "we have a problem. One of your bouncers just let an underage girl in here because she showed him her boobs."

"What! How do you know?" I asked him.

"Because I just happened to be standing close by and I saw him let her in, so I asked for her ID and she didn't have one. I know

July 1997: The Fiftieth Anniversary Motorcycle Rally

how careful you've been because you don't need any trouble with the cops."

"All the money I'm paying that security company and their guys are pulling that kind of crap? Which one is he?"

John pointed him out and I went after him like a crazy woman. I pulled him out in front of the bar by his collar and proceeded to rip him apart verbally at the top of my lungs in front of everyone, which amounted to quite a few people. I told him to get the hell off of my property and called his boss for a replacement. Ten minutes later my brother pulled me aside.

"Jeez, sis, I didn't think you were going to go that crazy. I know he blew it, but you just sent a six-foot-three-inch, two-hundred-and-fifty-pound man crying down the street, and I think you may have gotten him fired."

"It's my livelihood we're talking about here. He should have done his job. And now I'm sure none of the other guys will think about pulling a stunt like that."

"You're probably right about that, sis."

If I wasn't tending bar, telling someone what to stock or stocking it myself, getting change, or counting out tips so that I didn't run out of change, I was running around like the gestapo. I heard my name so many times from people who needed something from me that it echoed in my head. I'd set up tables outside of the building, where two good friends were selling my T-shirts, and if I wasn't needed in the bar I was needed out front. I was a frenzied crazy woman.

A few bikers from a notorious One Percent club were holding court at the end of my bar by the front door, and as I walked by I noticed one of them facing off with another man. The biker was a tall, large man who looked like a grizzly bear in a vest. He had never seen the wrath of the redhead before, and I never found the need to show him again. I got up underneath him and grabbed him by the vest to pull him down where he could hear me loud and clear, and I told him that I would not be having any fights in my establishment. I think he was in shock at first. He looked at me like I was a lunatic and then said in a calm voice, "I would never start a fight in your bar, lady." I think he was genuinely a nice guy, and my gumption was something he found funny as well as admirable. As packed as the bar was, no club member or biker started an altercation all weekend. I did, however, witness a lot of people behaving badly, and I'm sad to say it was usually the women who gave me trouble.

My aunt Joannie was pouring beer at the keg station close to the ladies' bathroom when she flagged me down. She has a funny way of saying things, and the way she delivered the information she shared with me kills me to this day.

"Charisse," she said to me, "I just overheard this fella that was getting a beer tell another guy that his girlfriend was in the men's room on the floor, and he told him that he could help himself to her."

"What? When did you hear that; what guy?"

"It was about ten minutes ago, but I had too many customers buying beer to tell you about it."

"The hell with the customers," I yelled as I raced to the men's room.

I kicked the door open and sure enough, there was a tall, leather-clad, dark-headed, drunken woman trying to get up off of the floor while pulling up her chaps and pants. I grabbed her arms and yanked her up and slammed her against the door, all the while screaming at her and telling her what a low-life piece of dirt she was. A man, who might have been her boyfriend or just another taker, pulled me off of her. I shoved her at him and yelled, "Get this bitch out of my building before I kill her." About that time my brother Jake happened along and escorted both of them out of the bar. I went back to the keg station and told my aunt that if she witnessed any more unacceptable behavior she was to drop everything immediately and find me or a bouncer.

I intervened as many women pulled up their shirts and rubbed their bare breasts in men's faces as well as against one another. Many wore tops that were cut to their navel, and flaunting boobs was routine. My so-called security company let people in the door who were already so drunk they couldn't see straight, and with customers piled four deep at the bar, it was impossible to see where all the drinks were going. We were relying heavily on the bouncers,

July 1997: The Fiftieth Anniversary Motorcycle Rally

who had nothing at stake but a paycheck and really didn't seem to care. I'm pretty sure my blood pressure never dipped below that of a prizefighter during a bout. With the possible exception of during my nightly three and half hours' sleep during that weekend, at which point it matched a triathlete's.

By Saturday night at eight o'clock, when Ray Wood and a few other officers came by, I was wondering how much more I could take. Ray promised me that he or one of his guys would walk me to my bank a half a block away on Saturday evening so that I could safely put some money into the night drop.

"Hey, Ray," I said. "How are you guys holding up?"

"It's crazy out there. We're having a lot of gang activity, and the streets are jammed and dangerous. They're all lined up waiting to get into your place, so we're going to need to have you close up for an hour."

"Close up for an hour. What the heck do you mean, close up for an hour? I thought you were here to take me to the bank?"

"If you need us to walk you to the bank, maybe you don't need to open back up."

"What kind of crap is that, Ray? I've been working my ass off. You told me you were going to walk me to the bank on Saturday and now you're telling me to close?"

"It's just for an hour, so we can get some of these people off of the street. We're not asking you, Charisse; we're telling you. Stop serving drinks now!"

"Fine," I said. "We'll close for an hour, but this whole thing makes no sense to me."

I went to Jeana behind the bar and told her what Ray said. I can't remember who was working with her, but they began to tell people that we had been told by the police department to close for an hour and that they would have to go, but that they were welcome to come back. It was eight p.m. on Saturday, July 3, 1997, and it was a night that Jeana and I will never forget. I was thoroughly exhausted and unnerved. This was something I never expected and wasn't quite sure how to handle.

"Don't worry, Charisse," Jeana said. "It will give us time to restock and put the place back together. You should go home and get some rest. You look wiped out. I've got your family here with me; we'll be fine. Go home now. I mean it; we're good."

"Okay, I know you're right. Look at the size of my ankles. They're so swollen they look like tree trunks, and they feel like they're about to explode."

"You've been on your feet for eighteen to twenty hours a day for the last four days. Our bodies weren't meant to take that kind of abuse. Now get the heck out of here," Jeana said.

I drove home in what felt like an altered state. I had thousands of dollars in beer boxes in my trunk because I was afraid to leave that much money at the bar, and I was scared to death that someone would stop me and try to take it. I made a wrong turn when leaving the bar, so Tommy didn't know where I was and I lost the comfort of his escort.

When I got home I threw myself on the couch with my huge ankles elevated and began to sob. I felt very close to a nervous breakdown. When Tommy came home I could see the helplessness in his face. He wanted badly to make me feel better, so he propped my legs up on top of pillows in bed, put ice packs on my ankles, and held me while I cried myself to sleep.

* * *

The next morning I was headed to the garage to get into my car and return to work when I saw my brother Bill coming out of the bathroom.

"Good morning. You guys were home early. You must have gotten out of the bar fast," I said.

"The cops never let us open back up, so we went to this place called the Office and sang karaoke for a while. We were home around midnight, I think," Bill said.

"What do you mean, they never let you open back up?"

"They kept us locked up in the bar for more than an hour, and said if we let anyone in you'd be closed for good. We cleaned the place up and restocked, and Jeana said we might as well go home. We saw the other bar on the way home and decided to stop in for an unwinder."

July 1997: The Fiftieth Anniversary Motorcycle Rally

"You must be kidding me! Do you have any idea how much money that cost me?"

I was so angry that I thought I would blow a blood vessel.

I got into my car and drove like a bat out of hell to the bar, almost daring a cop to stop me so I could tell him what I thought of the Hollister Police Department. When I got there the janitor was already finishing up.

"I can't believe how good the place looked this morning," she said. "After the mess I found yesterday I got here an hour early to make sure I would be done before seven, but it didn't look too bad."

"That's because we were closed at eight," I said with a grunt.

"Why would you close so early?" she asked.

I told her the sordid tale about the police department closing me down early.

"What can you do about it, though? They are the cops," she said.

"People have been calling me all weekend wanting an interview. I'll give them an interview. I'm calling KSBW. I'm going to let everyone know just how screwed-up law enforcement has been. They've got SWAT teams running around with rifles and gas masks, helicopters flying overhead every ten minutes, and cops walking around in packs of eight giving everyone the stink eye. What the hell is their problem? These are nice people who just want to spend money in our town and have a good time. The cops are treating everyone like criminals."

After making sure the bar was set up for another big day, I made a phone call to our local TV station, KSBW 8, and sure enough they were thrilled to come out and do an interview. I waited until ten a.m., when I thought Jeana would be up, and called her to get her version of what had transpired after I left Saturday night.

"I hope I didn't wake you," I said when she answered the phone.

"No, since I got home so early last night I was already up."

"Yeah, tell me what happened, Jeana?"

"Oh, Charisse, it was awful. At first I thought it was fine, because closing gave us the time to stock and clean up a little bit, and I figured that things would settle down as far as the crazies on the street go. But then the cops wouldn't let us open back up and it was just ugly."

"What do you mean by ugly?"

Jeana told me that one of the cops said if she unlocked the doors we would be closed for the rest of the weekend and maybe even fined. She said the guy was a real jerk, but she couldn't do anything about it, and that she didn't see the sense in waking me up. She knew my mouth, and she made the right call. I'm sure I would have been arrested.

"I appreciate that, Jeana. Did they close all the bars downtown?"

"No, just us, and all the crazy people outside the door were screaming at us to open. Women were up against the window with their tops up, pressing their boobs up against the glass. It was gross. I'm telling you. We kept yelling back that the cops wouldn't let us open, but no one would listen."

"Since the cops are the ones who told you not to open, why didn't they hang around to tell the people to go away? The bastards! I'm so mad I could spit bullets. I've called KSBW 8 and they're coming in for an interview. Man, are they going to get an earful."

"I know you're mad, but do you think it's a good idea to rip into law enforcement on television?"

"They can't get away with this crap, Jeana. They were supposed to give me an escort to the bank, and instead they shut me down, costing me thousands of dollars while they left all of the other bars open. It's just not right. I can't sit idly by and let them get away with it."

"I know you have to do what you feel is right, but just be careful, boss. We have to do business in this town long after the rally is over."

"I know, pal. Thanks for all your help. I'll see you at four. It sounds like everyone is rolling out today, so you should be out of here by eight or nine."

"I'll see you then."

July 1997: The Fiftieth Anniversary Motorcycle Rally

When I hung up with Jeana I was fighting mad. I was so angry that I wanted to slap somebody. I told everyone who would listen about how badly my staff had been treated and how much money the Hollister Police Department had cost me. It was against the fire code to have the building locked up with people inside, and I'd had fifteen people on payroll standing around.

I knew I needed to calm down and carry on. There were still many bikers in town, including our beloved Boozefighters. I was standing behind the bar feeling like I could drop over at any moment when a young girl came in and asked to talk to the owner.

I tentatively said, "I'm the owner. What can I do for you?"

"Hi, there," she said. "I'm Wino's granddaughter, and I wanted to bring you some of his ashes. This place meant so much to him, and I know that he would want a part of him to be left here. I've got his ashes with me, and if you can find something to put some in I'd like to leave some here with you."

I was overwhelmed and for a moment couldn't respond.

"Well, I can find something more appropriate later, but for now how about if we put some in a shot glass and cover it with cellophane wrap?"

"I think a shot glass is perfect. Gramps would like that."

I grabbed a shot glass and dashed to the kitchen for the cellophane, then joined Wino's granddaughter on the other side of the bar. The news media had gotten wind of the story and wanted to take pictures. When the shot glass was filled from the urn I carefully wrapped it and held it high, and a loud roar erupted: "Boozefighters up, here's to Willie." The room was filled with emotion and I began to cry. I couldn't tell you whether I was crying for Willie and his family or for myself. I was at such a point of exhaustion that a breakdown was imminent, and it seemed like a darn good time for one. The release of emotion gave me a second wind and made it easier to trudge through the final day.

* * *

Miracles and Grace in an Unlikely Place

PAYING TRIBUTE: Charise Tyson, co-owner of Johnny's Bar and Grill in Hollister, offers a toast with a shot glass containing ashes of the late 'Wino Willie' Forkner, who died just weeks before the 50th anniversary celebration of the 'Battle of Hollister.'

Biker legend 'returns' to Hollister

It finally slowed down enough for me to sit down and enjoy a much-needed beer, which went right to my head. Then the KSBW anchorman showed up for the interview. The bar was full of supporters who couldn't wait to see me tear into the police department on television. And I didn't disappoint. I railed on about how the cops shut me down while leaving all of the other bars open, therefore not getting anyone off of the streets, and leaving my crew to be terrorized. I told them how stupid our city council was to hire a fireman to be the combination police and fire chief, because he had no clue how to run a police department. I retold stories bikers shared with me about the way law enforcement was treating people. Tommy begged me not to do the interview. He agreed with Jeana and didn't want me to anger the police department and put ourselves at risk for retaliation. I didn't care. I was livid.

July 1997: The Fiftieth Anniversary Motorcycle Rally

Later, when the evening news aired, I was blown away by what I saw on the screen. I was filled with rage and looked like a raving lunatic. The entire bar cheered, but I found myself wishing that I had listened to my husband.

* * *

By five p.m. lots of the vendors had packed up, and many stopped in to thank us and say good-bye. "We hope to see you again next year," was a comment we heard repeatedly. "We hope to see you, too," we echoed back. By seven o'clock we were all dead on our feet, so we gave last call and closed the bar. I was grateful that I'd had the sense to close on Monday to get the place cleaned up and have the carpets shampooed. I headed home, thrilled that I was going to get a decent night's sleep for the first time in more than a week.

* * *

I crawled into bed to watch television, hoping that the TV would be enough of a distraction to stop the wheels in my head from turning, but my strategy failed. I continued to think about all of the things that I needed to do differently the following year to make things go more smoothly. I was rattling off all the things I wanted to remember when Tommy went and got me a tablet and a pen and told me to write them down and go to sleep. I did as he asked, and I vowed that things would be different next year.

I had no idea that the rally that brought more than a hundred thousand people with money to spend to our sleepy town would go on trial before the city council year after exhausting year to keep it alive—and would eventually be killed.

CLAMPERS, WIDDERS, & TRIATHLONS

Tommy and friends at a doin's

Clampers enjoying camrardie at Johnny's

WHAT SAY THE BRETHREN? SATISFACTORY!

Life was good as prominent business owners in a small town. Tommy and I were over the moon that the city's elite wanted to hang out at our bar and grill. John O'Brien shared many stories about Johnny's being the hub for business owners, farmers, city politicians, and more in the old days. It hadn't been that way for years. I couldn't have been prouder to be the one to bring Johnny's back to its days of grandeur.

* * *

One happy hour while visiting with our mayor, Seth Irish—who later became Tommy's best friend—Tommy discovered that Seth was a Clamper. Tommy decided it was only appropriate that we become an official Clamper bar. Tommy was initiated into the ECV in 1985, and had neglected his lifelong membership for quite some time. If our mayor was a Clamper, it was Tommy's duty to dust off the old red and black and honor the tradition.

Miracles and Grace in an Unlikely Place

"What the heck is a Clamper?" you may be asking, The E Clampus Vitus organization dates back to the early1800s and is rumored to have members of stature like Ulysses S. Grant, J. Pierpont Morgan, and even Ronald Reagan. Whether you choose to believe that is entirely up to you, but in their heyday they did a lot to help the widows and orphans of dead gold miners. The brotherhood was formed by men who thought organizations like the Odd Fellows and Masons were way too stuffy, and the requirements to join too arduous. As far as the ECV is concerned, all members are officers and as such are "all of equal indignity." New members, referred to as "Poor Blind Candidates," could present a "poke of dust," valued at the discretion of the brotherhood to join, and it wasn't uncommon for the fee to be waived if the man could not afford it.

The ECV are still responsible for building the historic-site plaques you see all over California, and I'm proud to say that one was erected on Johnny's patio to honor our own Wino Willie Folkner.

Wino's monument on Johnny's patio

What Say the Brethren? Satisfactory!

At Clamper doin's, as they are called, seasoned Clampers initiate new members and generally drink themselves into a stupor while playing crazy hazing games. For very good reasons, the initiations of new members are usually held in some remote place. They are weekend-long endeavors. The first time the men informed us that they would be out of town for the weekend, some of the women were bothered that their husbands wanted to leave them for two days. Party girl that I was, I saw it as a great opportunity for us "Widders," as we were referred to, to get together for a grand fiesta ourselves. The first weekend is etched in my memory and will be forever.

* * *

Allen was nineteen at the time and came to Hollister from San Jose, where he was living, for weekend visits. I informed him weeks in advance that he was going to be the designated driver for all of the Widders. Allen, always feeling it his duty to look out for ladies, possibly because he grew up with a single mom, had no problem with my plan.

The men headed out of town at three in the afternoon on Friday, and our party started before their vehicles left the parking lot. For two days we had more fun than the law should allow, and did everything from playing darts to holding a butt contest for the band members who played for us on Saturday night. When Tommy came home on Sunday morning he found me on the couch more hungover than he was, and our house was a disaster. We ran out of tomato juice for Bloody Marys, so I blended up Italian-style stewed tomatoes and tomato soup to make them. There was red stuff all over the kitchen and even in the hot tub. I don't remember ever having such a painful hangover in my life, and I had to drive Allen back to San Jose. I thought the ride might kill me, and on the drive my son said, "Mama, you girls told Allen things Allen didn't need to know." I forbade him to tell me what they were, and promised never to ask him to be designated driver for the Widders again.

THE WIDDERS' BALL

The Widders' Ball

When we embraced the ECV we added an entire new dimension to life at Johnny's. For a group of professional drinkers to call our bar home was a blessing in itself; the fun and camaraderie that came with it was an extra bonus. Most ECV chapters hold what they call a "Widders' Ball" once a year. It is the only party that we ladies are invited to attend. Clampers and Widders are encouraged to dress in period clothing for this extravaganza, and we turned finding our costumes into another party. We had so much fun picking out our outfits that we knew the ball was going to be a blast.

* * *

The night of the ball was, of course, another all-day party. Out of the hundred or so attendees at the event, about half dressed in period clothing, and our lively group from Hollister stood out in the crowd. We ate, laughed, danced, and drank until we were thrown out at midnight. The party moved to the hotel, and luckily the Clampers occupied the entire floor; we were a wild and crazy bunch. After room hopping for about an hour, we finally called it a night. The fart machine with a remote my husband sneaked into Seth and Jeannie's adjoining room made for another hour of entertainment. The next day we all went to brunch together, and any one of the attendees will surely tell you that it was one of the most fun weekends of his or her life.

THE JOHNNY'S TRIATHLON BEGINS

Triathlon photos from Ridgemark golf course.

The Johnny's Triathlon Begins

We made so many wonderful friends over the years, and each group brought a little more flavor and interest to our bar. Pauline Rivera, a good customer and great golfer, suggested we have a golf tournament, but because I don't golf I came up with the idea of a triathlon. This would not be your standard triathlon, with biking, swimming, and running. Our group was in no way qualified for that kind of physical activity. I decided we should play nine holes of golf—a scramble, so that I could play too—bowl three games—we had four teams of bowlers already in place—and finish back at Johnny's with three games of darts, followed by a barbecue. Everyone loved the idea, and plans for the First Annual Johnny's Bar & Grill Triathlon were birthed. The first year, we raised funds for our local YMCA.

Pauline handled all the golf details, and Cindi Bono, who had put on many bowl-athons for charity, handled the bowling end of the competition. I was left with not only the challenge of recruiting enough players to make the thing work, but the arduous job of collecting their money. I've organized many events over the years, and gathering the funds is always the part that makes me consider quitting and never arranging another one.

***

It took two months of planning, but we finally had everything in place. The prizes were collected, the fees for the bowling alley and the golf course were covered, and the food and volunteers for the barbecue taken care of. We were to tee off at Ridgemark Golf Course at six thirty in the morning. In typical Johnny's style I appeased the whiners who didn't want to start that early by having a bucket of Bloody Marys available at the first tee.

In preparation for the event, Tommy took me to the driving range to hit a few balls so I would at least know how to swing the club. Since we would all be hitting from the best ball, I figured I'd muddle through without embarrassing myself too badly. The swings and misses on the golf course were much more humiliating than the ones on the driving range. At least I gave everyone a good laugh.

We tried to put together teams with at least one good golfer, to keep things fair. Our strategy was to subtract the golf team score from individual bowling scores and add in the dart score for the winning total. People changed teams throughout, and went for the best individual score to determine who took first, second, and third places. We had some very diversified teams throughout the games. I found that I absolutely loved golf when I could move to the best golfer's ball and take my shot from there. I had fluorescent pink balls so I wouldn't lose them, and the most adorable powder-blue putter. You couldn't miss me out on the links.

Believe it or not, there are people who live on the golf course who like to sleep in past six thirty, and within two holes the golf superintendent tracked our group down to tell us to hold down the noise. I didn't want to have my group thrown off of the golf course on our first triathlon, so I begged people to quiet down. Bill Murray's got nothing on some of our clowns and their antics, and I thought I would die laughing. After golf we all headed back to Johnny's for a little breakfast before bowling.

The Johnny's Triathlon Begins

Many beers and Bloody Marys were consumed before we headed off to the bowling alley, which was fortunately only eight blocks away. It took us more than three hours to bowl three games, but, man, we had a ball. We were most likely one of the loudest groups the Hollister Bowling Alley had ever hosted. It should probably be illegal to have that much fun.

When we returned to Johnny's the barbecue awaited, and while everyone ate I tried to arrange for the final challenge of the games. It didn't take me long to figure out that three games of darts with a group that had been partying that long was way too many. One game was too many, in fact, and by my final triathlon event I had each contestant throw three darts.

Everyone had such a great time that before it was over they wanted me to plan another one. The annual event turned into biannual games, and the tradition continued for about five years. When our local bowling alley closed I was thrilled to have an excuse not to do another one. They were exhausting.

KIDS, KIDNEY STONES, AND BIG SURPRISES

KAT WITH A K SAVES THE DAY

I've introduced Jeana, who was with me from the start, but there are a few lovely ladies God blessed us with whom I haven't told you about yet. I was pretty much at my wits' end when Kat arrived on the scene in November of 1999. She was a cute, tiny little thing with long blond hair that fell way past her backside, and you would never believe that she was the mother of three boys. She had loads of experience and was honest to a fault. In the previous year I'd hired and fired five bartenders for the spot she filled, and when her honesty and integrity matched Jeana's I was thrilled. She wasn't an easy person to get to know, but once people got past her tough exterior they found a lamb of a lady who would look out for them and defend them to the death.

Kat had been working for me for a short time when Jeana informed me that she would need some time off because she was pregnant. Jeana was just as shocked as I was, because she was almost forty and wasn't planning on having more children. God blessed her with a boy who was the light of her life, and she returned to work only a month after she gave birth. A while later, when Kat asked to speak to me about something important, I said, "As long as you don't tell me you're pregnant," and she walked off. When I asked where she was going, she said, "You told me not to tell you I was pregnant." She, too, was almost forty, and hadn't exactly planned on having another child. She was blessed with another boy to add to her clan of three, and returned to work about three weeks later. I had a hearty crew.

MISS SYLVIA

One of Tommy's favorite haunts was Dona Esters Mexican restaurant in neighboring San Juan Bautista. We both liked to eat there on weekends before we bought the bar. After we bought Johnny's it became one of the places Tommy went to drink, away from my watchful eye. His favorite bartender was Sylvia. We hired her to tend bar during the 1998 rally and she worked three of them before we hired her to work full time in December of 2000. I needed more time to take care of business affairs and she was the perfect fit. She took over some of the tedious tasks like ordering bar supplies. She also became my secretary and my technician. She reminded me of the many things my overloaded brain forgot and was the only one that could reset the cash register of fix the soda dispenser when it acted up. She was kind and motherly and took all of the lost and lonely characters that wandered into Johnny's under her wing.

ENTER WOO

Wendy just kind of appeared at Johnny's. She came in so quietly that I couldn't tell you exactly when she showed up, although I believe it was somewhere in the middle of 2002. Thursdays had been off the hook for a while, and after my ten-hour bartending shift, helping Jeana keep up behind the bar until two in the morning was taking a toll on me. Wendy had been a customer for a short time when she asked Jeana whether we needed any help. Jeana told her about our crazy Thursday nights and said that she would talk to me about hiring her for a Thursday night second bartender. I took Jeana up on her suggestion and added Wendy to the crew, and it worked out beautifully. Now I could bar back and sit down in between, and the girls could concentrate on pouring drinks: more pouring, and more cha-ching.

 Wendy is a blond beauty with the disposition of an angel. In her mid-forties, she became the most senior woman in the bevy. Once again God blessed me with a woman of integrity. She became our fill-in and help-out girl. She started cleaning the bar, and her work ethic carried over into that job, too. No one had ever cleaned the bar the way she did. She was always there when we needed her; she fit in well and completed our family.

*　*　*

In 2006, a pretty rough year, while I was dealing with many extra challenges, like finding a decent cook and fretting that my alcoholic husband would be hurt or arrested while driving around intoxicated, tragedy struck our Woo. To this day I will never know how she got through the assault on her health. She got a weird disease that caused her hands and sometimes her face to swell up. When she got through that, she wound up with a huge kidney stone and she was admitted to the hospital many times before they could blast it to pieces. When it became impossible for her to work, a really wonderful customer and friend, Annie, stepped in to clean the bar. Kat covered her bartending shift, and a great group of customers came together and hosted a benefit to keep Wendy afloat. Wendy is a proud woman and didn't want any handouts, but with no choice left she came to accept our gifts with dignity and grace. There is nothing like finding out how much you are loved by those around you to lift your spirits, and our Woo needed all the help we could give in that area.

The crew of regular customers who came to call themselves "the Varsity" facilitated more benefits at Johnny's than I can even count. They were a close-knit bunch of guys whom I would liken to a high school girls' clique. If you weren't one of them, they might let you hang out for a while, but they never let you get too comfortable. As gruff as they were, they knew how to throw a benefit barbecue, and when our very own Woo needed help they were right there. Besides putting on a very successful barbecue that helped her financially, they drove her to doctors' appointments, bought her groceries, and brought her laughter in the midst of her misery. For that I will always be grateful.

WHAT DO YOU MEAN, YOU DON'T OWN A MOTORCYCLE?

Leaving the Scottsdale, Arizona, Harley-Davidson dealer on our new Road King

Miracles and Grace in an Unlikely Place

As we were owners of a biker bar, people assumed that Tommy and I had a motorcycle. Every time we said that we didn't own one, we took a ton of flak. Tommy hadn't ridden a motorcycle in decades, and had never acquired a license to ride one, so he signed up for the motorcycle safety training course in Gilroy. He got his license and we kept our eyes out for a good deal on a used Harley, but we really hadn't been doing much shopping until we wound up in the Harley-Davison dealership in Scottsdale, Arizona.

* * *

We had gone to Phoenix for my mother's biker wedding, and we rented a Heritage Softail to ride while we were there. I thought it was a pretty comfortable ride, but Tommy was drawn to the Road King. We went to the Scottsdale dealership to look around, not intending to buy anything, and I spotted a 1996 green Road King. The color of the bike was exactly the same as the green in our Johnny's logo, and I was in love. We took it out for a test drive, and on returning I told Tommy that we just had to have it. He thought I was a bit crazy, because he was the one who would have to drive us from Phoenix to Hollister in late November with our luggage strapped to the bike. It wasn't until I went to get my motorcycle license seven years later that I realized just how cruel and selfish it was to inflict that ride on my poor husband. I canceled our airline tickets, and Mom took us out shopping for a little bit of motorcycle gear. We had absolutely nothing to prepare us for the long journey. There was no helmet law in Arizona, so we didn't have any of those. Even in late November the weather was pretty nice, so we didn't have any warm clothes.

There was no way we were going to make it back to Johnny's for the Lights on Parade, but my crew assured me that they would get it handled. I worried incessantly about it, but I wanted my motorcycle, and that took precedence. We planned on taking two days to make the trip, with a stop somewhere around Bakersfield.

* * *

What Do You Mean, You Don't Own a Motorcycle?

Calling it the trip from hell doesn't get close to describing it. We bought a T-bag, and the bike had two hard saddlebags, which we bungee-wrapped our extra bags to. We managed to get our entire luggage on the bike. Fortunately I'm a light packer, and I travel with only carry-on luggage whenever possible, but that was one loaded-down Harley. Driving the motorcycle by itself that distance would have been hard enough for Tommy, but adding me and our luggage to it was insane.

After praying for our safety, we headed out bright and early Saturday morning. We had no MapQuest or GPS. We just took off with loose directions and hoped for the best. We accidently wound up taking some back roads, but by a miracle we wound up in Barstow at six o'clock at night. The ride was cold, the wind blew hard, and we were exhausted. Our butts were so sore we could barely walk. Since we weren't seasoned riders, we had to make quite a few pit stops to rest our backsides; hence the eight-hour journey.

We found a Super 8 motel with a restaurant within walking distance, and after a quick meal I soaked in a hot bath, and Tommy hit the bed. We slept like logs, and dreaded getting on the road again. It was cold when we headed out, but we had no idea how cold it was going to get. The temperature on the Tehachapi was about fifty-eight degrees, and if you threw in the windchill factor it was close to freezing. I kept my head buried in Tommy's back, and when the semis drove by I thought they were going to blow us off of the road. When we hit Bakersfield our hands and feet were so frozen that we felt like they could crack, and our noses felt like they were going to chip right off of our faces. We hobbled into a restaurant, and I knew no matter what we ordered off the menu, I was eating a heaping helping of humble pie. We sat in silence with our hands around our coffee cups until our lips thawed out enough to speak.

"I am so sorry, honey," I said through chattering teeth. "I had no idea it would be this bad. I don't know what else to say. I don't blame you if you want to kill me. I deserve it."

"I should kill you," Tommy said. "You're so damn stubborn. You have to have and do everything *right now*. I hope you've learned something from this experience."

"I learned that my honey is the strongest and most wonderful man on the face of the earth. I don't know how you kept the bike upright."

"Keep kissing up, but you're going to owe me for a very long time. My hands were frozen solid, and I couldn't even turn the wheel to get off of the freeway. I didn't think I was going to make it."

"I know, honey. I'll try to make it up to you. I promise."

"You bet you will."

We ate our meal, and Tommy drank three cups of coffee and I drank as much hot tea. We dreaded getting back on the road, so we lingered for about an hour.

"It's already going to be dark by the time we get home," Tommy said. "The worst part should be behind us now, but we'd better get going."

Fortunately it warmed up a bit for the next leg of the trip. We stopped at a bar somewhere off of Highway 33 to have a couple of drinks, and I called Johnny's and told them that we were about two and half hours out. Kat said we had a bunch of people waiting to see us ride in, so we'd better not go straight home. I tiptoed around telling Tommy that I wanted him to stop at the bar, but when I did he shocked me by agreeing to it without a problem. He did say that we weren't staying, just stopping.

By the time we hit Hollister it was really cold once again. Someone was out in front of Johnny's having a cigarette as we pulled up, and he ran in and called for the gang. We showed up to such a cheering crowd that you would have thought we were rock stars. Our friends made us feel so good that it almost made the entire trip worth it. I did say almost. . . .

What Do You Mean, You Don't Own a Motorcycle?

Glad to be home with our waiting entourage

LIFE WAS A PARTY; THEN I WOKE UP

IGNORING THE PROBLEM IN FRONT OF MY FACE

Our best friends, Seth and Jeannie, decided to get married in Jamaica. I arranged for a large group from Johnny's to make the trip to share in their joyous occasion. I was really looking forward to some downtime away from Johnny's. Things had been pretty dicey between Tommy and me for quite a while, and I'd hoped that the tropical location, wedding, and great suite would put a little fire back into our relationship. Unfortunately, at this point Tommy's drinking was taking quite a toll on our love life, and my unrealistic expectations only pressured him and made intimacy even more difficult.

Thankfully I had lots of friends to hang out with when he passed out early. He went to the room and I stayed out and partied with our pals every night; so much for romance. As it turned out, it was the beginning of the end, and I didn't even see it coming. I was so wrapped up in my accomplishment of putting together such a great trip that I failed to notice that when my husband wasn't

Ignoring the Problem in Front of My Face

sloshed, he was just plain miserable. As long as my friends were enjoying their honeymoon I was happy.

* * *

Life at the bar had been such a party that it was easy to dismiss how serious Tommy's drinking problem had become. One party rolled into the next, and I selfishly enjoyed getting drunk with my husband during one of our soirees or while on vacation. At the same time I wanted him to step up and be my helper, but he just wasn't capable of it. I could be three sheets to the wind, and if a party of twenty people walked through the door I would snap out of it, make drinks, wash glasses, and sell T-shirts, practically on autopilot. If a job needed to be done I got it done, and I got it done now. I was incapable of walking past a dirty table or a sink full of dishes without cleaning it up. I could take care of business.

Tommy is a procrastinator by nature. You throw alcoholism into the mix and he wasn't getting much done, and it certainly wasn't getting done fast enough for me. So I did everything myself. My husband got so used to me handling things that he pretty much stopped helping me at all. If there were cases of water that needed to be put away, he let me lift them. If the pilot light went out on the water heater, I fired it up again.

It didn't take employees long to figure out that if they left things alone long enough, I would put them away, clean, or stock them. They assumed that they wouldn't do things the way I wanted them done anyway, so they just left them for me to deal with. I took care of everything, because it was just easier that way. The lesson I learned as a child helping to raise my brothers—if you want it done right, do it yourself—stayed with me. I was a good person to have on your team if you wanted something done, but as the owner of a small business it was exhausting.

I was your classic enabling codependent. The less others did, the more I took care of, all the while complaining about it. Nagging my husband certainly wasn't helping to get things done. I didn't keep my complaints to myself either. Everyone in the bar got to hear me drone on about my good-for-nothing husband. It wasn't long before they were talking badly about him, too. They knew that it was practically impossible to get him to fix anything that was broken, and customers started offering to fix things for me. They did electrical work, plumbing, and even carpentry work. They fixed bar stools, stereos, tables, and chairs.

My disrespect for Tommy got so bad that I ignored him unless I was telling him about something that needed to be done. I was in a perpetual angry state, and it took very little to set me off. I snapped at my employees for the smallest mistakes. When blunders were made I just couldn't let them go. If something an employee did made extra work for me, I went on about it for days at a time.

***

I remember the day that Jeana blasted me in desperation. She was always respectful, and it took quite a bit to get her angry, so I must have really been getting to her. I don't even remember what I was going on about, but it was probably something trivial. I most likely made a snide remark about the fact that no one ever did what I asked, and Jeana blew a gasket.

"All right already," she screamed. "So we're not perfect. We're human and we make mistakes. You never notice the things we do right, but God forbid we don't put something where you like it. Nothing is ever good enough for you, so either fire us or shut up about it."

She spun around with a flip of her hair and went back to work. I was in complete shock. If it had come from anyone else I would have been livid, but Jeana was my rock. From the beginning she was our sunshine girl. She stayed upbeat and positive and always found the good in people. A battle brewed inside of me. I knew I should apologize to her, but I couldn't stop thinking about the little things she left undone that drove me crazy. I couldn't admit to myself that my way wasn't always the best way. I didn't want to accept the fact that a lot of the things that drove me crazy—like the staff not stocking the straws, napkins, and coasters—were not that

Ignoring the Problem in Front of My Face

big a deal in the scheme of things. I couldn't stand being wrong, and at that point in my life I very seldom admitted that I was.

I found the negative in every situation. I didn't like being that way, but it seemed to be a part of my DNA. I used to hate the fact that no matter how hard I tried to keep my mother happy by taking care of the house, she would find something wrong or just not notice at all. Now I was doing the same thing myself. Somewhere along the line in dealing with my husband's disease I'd become a person that I didn't like. I'd been a control freak as far back as I could remember, but lately I'd been over-the-top. I got irritated on a dime and pretty much stayed that way all day. And the opportunities to get peeved came in bucketloads. If one thing went wrong it started a snowball of events that overtook me on a regular basis. What can go wrong will go wrong, and if you are looking for problems and expecting them, that's precisely what you are going to get.

* * *

A DISINTEGRATING MARRIAGE AND A WARPED MIND

Our marriage was already strained, and certain events pushed it right over the edge. I'd started throwing a customer-appreciation party every year on Labor Day weekend after the successful 1997 rally. Most of our customers hung out at Johnny's seven days a week, and during the rally there was never room for them. I figured the folks who kept us going all year long deserved a thank-you, so I closed the bar the Sunday before Labor Day and invited everyone to our house for a barbecue. I worked for days getting the house and yard ready for the party. I went a bit over-the-top: buying new lawn furniture and plants, cleaning every nook and cranny that was just going to get dirty during the party, and stocking the fridge with enough food, beer, and wine for an army. I'd ask Tommy to get sand for the ashtrays, sweep out the garage, or haul garbage to the dump, and he got so ugly I wanted to slap him. We fought for at least a week because of the party. When it finally arrived everyone played Ping-Pong, horseshoes, darts, and poker. We sang, danced, laughed and had a great time—everyone but Tommy, that is.

* * *

It seemed like we fought about everything. We'd stopped holding hands and telling each other "I love you." We didn't spend any quality time together, not even a dinner date. A testament to how screwed-up in the head I was is how angry I got that we weren't having sex anymore. We didn't even like each other, and I thought we should be having sex. In some warped part of my brain I equated having sex with being loved. It may have had something to do with my past abuses, but whatever the reason, I figured as long as Tommy and I were still doing it, he still loved me despite the way he was treating me. Though I didn't understand it at the time, this distorted view opened up a huge door for the devil to mess with my mind.

I became obsessed with sex. I tried everything to get Tommy interested in it. I bought a crazy swing that hung from the bedroom ceiling, and assorted toys, lotions, and creams, and even got into X-rated movies. I ordered the adult channels from the cable company and turned them on almost nightly to try to get my husband warmed up for intimacy. At first he went along with me and tried to pretend he was into it, but the truth was, it wasn't his thing. It shouldn't have been mine either, but a warped mind confused by dysfunction and past abuses was easily deceived. I know now that Satan was using my insecurities to turn me inside out.

Consuming two fifths of alcohol every day will have a profound effect on a man's sexual drive, and our love life was pretty much in the tank. I didn't blame the alcohol, though; I blamed myself. I made Tommy's problem all about me. If I were in better shape he might want me more, I told myself. I tried desperately to lose weight; I was about twenty pounds heavier than I should have been. I walked and exercised for almost two hours, four days a week, but I couldn't drop a pound. And Tommy compounded my insecurities with very hurtful comments.

* * *

I had problems with indigestion and had taken Prevacid for years. If I neglected to take my pill, a glass of water sent me over the edge in pain, so my doctor suggested I have some tests done. An upper GI confirmed that I had a hole in my esophagus that would require surgery to repair. It was a pretty routine procedure, and it was very possible that I would lose some weight as a result of it. *Oh, happy days,* I thought. *No more heartburn, and I finally lose the weight that I can't seem to take off.* I couldn't wait to tell Tommy about it.

He had been out golfing with one of his buddies, and they stopped in the lounge for cocktails afterward, so he was pretty well lit when he got home.

"Honey, I got the results from my tests and had my meeting with the doctor today," I told him. "I have a hole in my esophagus and I'm going to need some surgery. It's not real serious, but I will be out of commission for a few days. The great news is that he said a lot of people who have the surgery lose twenty pounds."

"Great," he said. "Maybe then I can get a hard-on."

It was one of the cruelest and most damaging things he could have said to me. I already felt like I was undesirable because our sex life had so deteriorated, and that comment went right to the core of my insecurities. I ran to our bedroom crying, and Tommy didn't even know what he'd said. When he came to the bedroom door I told him to go to hell and sleep on the couch. The pain of that comment was so intense that it felt like a hot dagger had been shoved into my heart.

Of course, the next morning Tommy didn't even remember why he was sleeping on the couch, but I cried all night, and I was even more convinced that our lack of a sex life was because of my weight. None of the diets I tried were helping. The drinks I was throwing back may have had a little something to with it. I'd started drinking a lot more than I should, in self-defense. If I had to go home to a drunk every day, I wasn't going to do it sober. I started staying later and later at the bar. I very seldom cooked a meal for my husband anymore, and I was pretty bad about eating one myself. I drank dinner at least four nights a week. I couldn't even see the depths of my dysfunction.

A Disintegrating Marriage and a Warped Mind

Deserted by my father at a young age, I kept up my battle for approval by the opposite sex. Since our love life was in the tank and Tommy wasn't one for paying compliments even when he did like me, my wounded ego caused me to tolerate and even welcome advances from male customers. There was one particular customer who had it bad for me. We shook dice for drinks for hours almost daily, and he knew that once I'd had enough cocktails I wouldn't notice his hand on my butt or his arm brushing one of my breasts. If I'm honest about it, once I got drunk I stirred him on, because it felt good to feel wanted. Like I said, my mind was twisted. I was a wounded soul looking for acceptance.

I began tolerating behavior from the regulars that I should never have put up with, much less encouraged. There was a certain group of regulars who constantly made sexual innuendoes and used the F-bomb incessantly, and I used it myself on a pretty regular basis. They made degrading comments and jokes about my husband, and instead of defending him I laughed right along with them. I was one of them. I was part of the crew. I'd lost all perspective of right and wrong. I wore low-cut blouses in an effort to get even more attention. If someone patted my butt while I was sober I would slap his hand and say, "What the heck do you think you're doing?" But while intoxicated I paid no attention to someone grabbing it. I was a walking contradiction.

We use cameras at the bar to keep an eye on things when we're at home, and Tommy witnessed more groping than any man should have to bear. He'd call me on it when I got home, and I'd make light of it and tell him that it wasn't that bad. I'd tell him that at least someone thought I was sexy. Then I'd make some snide remark that bashed his manhood. This, of course, would lead to his making a nasty comment about me. We had some knock-down drag-outs, especially when we were both drunk. I remembered every nasty and snide remark Tommy made to me in his drunken state. I filed them away in my memory banks and pulled them out at will.

The nasty things I said to him were always an assault on his manhood. I wielded a pretty mean sword with my tongue. And Tommy was easy pickin's. After all, he was a drunk and he didn't work. He said stupid things to customers when he was drunk, and insulted them. I'd called Johnny's *my* bar for so long that he resented it wildly. People would call him Tom Tyson, which sent him over the edge. He figured that if it was my bar, I could take care of it without his help. He was so embittered by it that he made a scene if I asked him to replace a washer in the faucet. The disrespect from me and many customers finally grew to an intolerable state, and that was when he snapped.

* * *

    I'd asked him to go to therapy with me because I wanted to save our marriage; he went because he wanted a divorce. Since it wasn't hard to talk him into going, I took it to be a good sign, but the joke was on me. I think he agreed to go so that he could tell me we were finished in front of a professional counselor. The shock was almost more than I could take. I didn't understand how he could want to leave me. I'd been taking care of him for years. I felt like I'd been taking care of others my entire life: my brothers, my son, and now my husband. I had responsibilities. If I didn't take care of business our bills didn't get paid and our employees wouldn't have paychecks. Why didn't anybody cut me some slack once in a while? I was having one hell of a pity party. I'd been doing that a lot lately. I'd somehow changed from a happy- go- lucky and fun-loving person into a whining and complaining bitch.

    I ignored God completely unless I wanted Him to do something for me. I never equated my problems with something that I might be doing. The devil had been remarkably deceitful. The metamorphosis of my entire personality had taken place a little at a time, so slowly, in fact, that I hadn't even noticed it. Don't get me wrong: I knew I was a control freak, but I always thought of myself as a caring and giving person. I enjoyed helping people, and put their needs ahead of my own often. I thought I was a pretty good person, but I had some serious soul-searching to do. There is nothing like the threat of losing someone you've invested thirteen years of your life with to knock you for a loop and make you ask yourself the hard questions.

THE D-WORD, AL-ANON, HEALING, AND GRACE

THIS CAN'T BE HAPPENING TO ME

The reality was harsh: My husband wanted a divorce. I was completely devastated. In desperation I screamed out to God, "Why is this happening to me? I'm a good person. What did I do to deserve this?" God's still, small voice said: *You knew your husband was an alcoholic and you bought a bar. What did you think was going to happen?* I wasn't really expecting to hear an answer to my question, and I certainly did not like the one that I received. My mother raised my three brothers and me as Christians. I knew very well who Jesus was and loved Him very much, but I paid no attention to Him unless I was praying for His help to get over a hangover or things were falling apart.

I accepted Jesus and was baptized at the age of nine, but had all but abandoned my Christian roots long ago. The farther from God I got, the easier it was to justify the things I did that I knew deep down were not pleasing to Him. When I thought really hard about it, I had been making excuses for my behavior for a very long time. But I still did not believe that I deserved to be dumped by the man I had been taking care of for so many years.

I thought about Mom. I knew she would understand my pain. She was on her fifth marriage. She'd made some pretty poor

This Can't Be Happening to Me

choices when it came to men, but had been with her current husband a little longer than I had been with Tommy. I loved my mother, but I did not want to follow in her footsteps in the marriage department. I always swore that I would never get a divorce. Maybe that was why I hung in there for so long. I wasn't a quitter, and I hated to lose. I hadn't been happy in my marriage for years, but the thought of it ending was more than I could take. I dialed Mom and was relieved that she picked up the receiver.

"Hi, Mom," I said.

"Charissey, what's wrong?" Mom always called me Charissey when she felt I needed mothering, and my voice told her in an instant that I was upset. "Tommy wants a divorce," I wailed.

"Oh, Charissey, no!"

"I can't believe it, Mom. After all I've done. I've been paying all of the bills and taking care of everything since we bought the bar. He's hardly worked a day since he quit his job in March of 1996. And God forbid I ask him to fix something at the bar or at the house. I ask him to put a new battery in the smoke detector and you'd think I'd asked him for a kidney. And he wants to divorce me?"

"Maybe he is just upset right now and he isn't thinking straight."

"Damn right he isn't thinking straight. How the hell does he think he's going to take care of himself? I've been paying for his gas, truck registration, and insurance. Where will he live, and how will he pay rent? This is insane, Mom. What the heck am I going to do?"

"Do you still love him?"

Mom raised a good question. I was beginning to think that I didn't anymore, but the thought of losing Tommy was debilitating. He was the only man who I felt truly loved me and would never cheat on me. I just wanted him to be a good husband and for us to work things out, and I told my mother so. She reassured me as much as she could and told me to get some rest before we hung up.

I reminisced about the way we used to be. We were always kissing and holding hands. How long had it been since we were like that? We slept in the same bed but hadn't touched each other in quite some time. We used to spoon every morning for ten minutes before getting out of bed. I'd wrap myself around Tommy and press my breasts into his back and he would practically purr. It was a ritual we had long since abandoned.

Then there was the damn sex thing; I had been complaining so much about that lately. I was a complete contradiction of emotions. How could I be so angry with Tommy all the time, and still want to have sex with him? If I didn't initiate it we wouldn't do it at all, and the rejection had become more than I could take. It felt like I was asking him to eat nails, not make love. I missed all of the warm and wonderful feelings that used to go along with it. The toys and the X-rated movies I'd incorporated only made me feel dirty now.

What had I become? How had I lost myself so completely? It was clear that I needed help. I needed to get to one of those Al-Anon meetings right away. I didn't think it would be a good idea to go to one in Hollister. My bar was probably the place many attendees' significant others went to for their daily fix. A meeting out of town seemed like a better idea. I went on the Internet and found an eleven a.m. meeting in Morgan Hill. I would be there the next day come hell or high water.

***

I didn't get much sleep that night. Tommy stayed on the couch and I cried and slept intermittently. He got up and had his "start my day" screwdriver at about six thirty a.m., took a shower, and left the house.

Facing the possibility of a divorce was draining. I had the strength of a kitten and didn't want to leave my bed. I felt like staying under the covers and crying indefinitely. The sensible part of me knew I needed to get up and get to the Al-Anon meeting. I lay in bed for what felt like an eternity, the pathetic me battling with the rational me, and rational finally won out. I got up, showered, and dressed almost on autopilot. I headed to Johnny's and ducked in the back door and headed upstairs before anyone could see me.

This Can't Be Happening to Me

Lately talking to people brought me to tears, and my sore, burning eyes needed a break. I took care of my necessary business and headed out to find my meeting.

I wasn't exactly sure where I was going, and I have a terrible sense of direction, so an early departure seemed like a good idea. I arrived at the address and found that the meeting was being held at what looked like an old church that was no longer in use. The building was in a state of disrepair. Its white paint was chipped and washed out, and the doors looked like they could fall off the hinges at any moment.

When I arrived I was greeted by an older lady, and she, too, looked like she had seen better days. I wondered how many years with an alcoholic attributed to her rough appearance. She was thin as a rail, with stringy gray hair and clothes that looked like they had been purchased at a Goodwill store long ago. She was kind and soft-spoken. She welcomed me and informed me that their meetings had been pretty small lately.

Within ten minutes a woman who looked to be in her mid-fifties and a gentleman of about sixty arrived. We began the meeting by introducing ourselves, as I learned is always done at Al-Anon meetings. "Hello, my name is so-and-so, and I am a codependent." The meeting was so uneventful and drab that I have trouble even remembering what was said. I knew that this was not the place for me. I thanked the very nice people and said my farewells, and when they said they hoped to see me next week, I politely said, "We'll see what happens."

The day was still young, so I went back to work to see whether I could concentrate on getting some book work done. Once again I sneaked in the back door and up to my office. I avoided the caring customers who would have wanted to know how I was doing. Until I was capable of talking to people who cared about me without crying, I was going to avoid conversations completely. I took care of a little business and then went online to find a different Al-Anon meeting. There was one in San Jose on Blossom Hill Road in a church that my family attended when I was about ten years old. I figured that was a sign. The meetings were on Mondays and Wednesdays at seven p.m. I could have a nice visit with my aunt while I was in town and then go on to my meeting.

***

I headed home to see what awaited me. Tommy wasn't around, so I curled up with a book and read myself to sleep. I couldn't listen to the radio or watch TV. I liked two kinds of music: country and western. That music will make you cry even if your marriage isn't falling apart. None of my usual shows held any interest to me. I sat and thought a lot. I remembered how happy Tommy and I once were. I refused to believe that he didn't love me anymore. I knew with every fiber of my being that he still did.

"Oh, Lord, help me figure this thing out," I prayed. "I don't want to be a divorcée. Where did we go so wrong?"

Tommy was right: Things had been bad for a long time. I worried about Tommy getting a DUI, and yet I'd gotten into the habit of getting pretty tipsy before driving home so that I could tolerate my husband. Oh, the ugly arguments we had when we were both drunk. I hated thinking about the nasty things we said to each other. When was the last time I'd fixed him a meal? I used to love to make a nice dinner for my man. I thought that sitting down together to enjoy a meal was a good opportunity to discuss important issues, but Tommy said I ruined his appetite. It also got to where he couldn't remember the next day what he'd eaten the day before, and there was a lot of spillage during the meal, so I just gave up.

At least Tommy was still eating a good meal or two at the bar every day. I believed that my old pal Danny's lack of interest in food accelerated his demise. We'd be out on the town partying and Danny wouldn't even think about food until I mentioned that I was starving. We'd order something to eat, but he always left most of his food on his plate. Danny died of cirrhosis in 2000 and I was really rough on Tommy. I said, "If you think I'm going to watch you kill yourself you are seriously mistaken." How long ago had I said that? Now here I was supporting my husband's habit while he poured two liters of booze down his throat every single day, and that was only what he consumed at home. Man, I needed help.

* * *

Tommy came home and headed to our bedroom so that he could watch television and not be in the same room with me. When I went into our room he headed to the couch to sleep. His not sleeping in our bed wasn't anything new. He had been passing out on the couch most nights now. I stopped trying to get him to come to bed. The smell of stale Jack Daniel's permeated the room when he was in it. It was like he was being pickled from the inside out. It was strange, though. When he wasn't next to me in bed there was always sadness inside of me, a terrible feeling of loss. How could one person have so many conflicting feelings? I grabbed my stuffed rabbit, buried my face in its stomach, and cried myself to sleep.

* * *

I woke up on the Wednesday after Tommy asked me for a divorce and decided that I couldn't let my body and my mind both go to pot. I did about ten minutes of one of my exercise videos and some stretching and headed out for my one-hour walk. I knew the fresh air and exercise would do me good, even though I was a little weak. I found it hard to eat after Tommy dropped the bomb on me. The good news was that I was losing weight, although this wasn't a diet I would recommend to my worst enemy.

The air was crisp and clean. The cold felt good on my face. I had been crying so much that my face and eyes constantly burned. Tommy was going about his business like nothing had even happened. The only difference was that he never came to bed anymore. I was beginning to wonder whether he felt anything. I was falling apart and he seemed completely oblivious. The more I thought about it, the madder I got. Mad felt a lot better than hurt, so I decided to stay that way. When I'm mad I walk fast. That day I shaved twelve minutes off of my usual time to complete my walk. I got home, showered, and headed to work.

Miracles and Grace in an Unlikely Place

When I arrived, Sylvia asked whether I had eaten anything—always the mother, my Sylvia. I told my cook that I would try a piece of wheat toast with a couple slices of bacon on it. Our bacon is so good I could eat it in a coma. My crew told me that I looked a little better, which brought me back to tears. The poor things never knew what to say to me. I took care of some business and told Syl I was headed to San Jose for a visit with my aunt. She was glad that I was getting out of town.

* * *

I arrived at Joannie's house and was greeted with a nice warm hug, which, of course, brought me to tears.

"How have you done it, Joannie?" I asked. "You've been putting up with Uncle Mike's addiction for what has to be forty years. Heck, you divorced him and then remarried him. What are you, crazy?"

"I love your uncle. I don't like the man he has become because of his drinking. He was really a good man at one time. I suppose deep down he still is. He will drink himself to death one day, if the cancer doesn't take him first, or the emphysema. He still smokes, too."

We spent a while talking about how our men used to be and how sad we were that booze had become the most important thing in their lives. Then Aunt Joannie asked if I would watch a video with her.

"Have you ever heard of Joyce Meyer?" she asked.

"No, I can't say that I have."

"You'll love her. She's a straight shooter. She reminds me of you in a lot of ways."

The woman in the video was dressed in a stylish yet unpretentious outfit. She looked to be in her early fifties. She had a very low voice. She spoke with authority and gentleness at the same time. The subject of the video was codependency. I'd heard the word before, but never gave it a lot of thought.

"Are you codependent?" she asked. "If someone else's problem controls your behavior, your happiness, or your life decisions, you suffer from codependency."

This Can't Be Happening to Me

Wow! That was a shot between the eyes. If I wasn't the poster girl for codependency, I didn't know who was. Joyce asked more questions that hit home:

"Are you controlling and manipulative?

"Do you spend your life trying to rescue and fix other people?

"Do you feel like a failure because you can't help someone in your life?

"Do you have a false sense of responsibility?

"Are you exhausted from trying to run the whole world?

"Are you so entangled in someone else's life that it has taken over your own life?"

Holy crap, this lady was killing me. And she wasn't finished yet.

Everything she said made sense: "You can't help someone until they are ready to be helped. Stop letting someone ruin your life because they don't want to enjoy theirs. Stop wearing yourself out trying to do something that you can't do anything about. You can't change people or yourself. Only God can change people." She shared what a miserable person she had been for many years. She suffered sexual abuse as a child at the hands of her father. She explained that a person who has no control over the injustices suffered at the hands of others, especially those who should have been looking out for them can come to believe that they have to control everything and everyone around them in order to keep from getting hurt. She shot arrow after arrow into my heart. Joyce said that her husband, Dave, refused to let her steal his joy. He actually asked God to give him a woman who needed help. According to Joyce, he might have gotten a little more than he had bargained for. She said that her husband let her have her own way for quite a while into their marriage before God told him it was time to confront her. Dave told her that he was never going to be able to make her happy and that he was through trying. It was verbatim what Tommy had said to me two days earlier.

I saw the video as divine intervention. I needed to get to my Al-Anon meeting, so I asked Joannie if I could borrow the videotapes. I really wanted to watch them at home alone so I could blubber in privacy. My aunt told me that she knew I would like Joyce, and she very gladly sent the videos home with me, as well four sets of cassette tapes that I could listen to while I drove.

*　*　*

As soon as I got into my car I put in one of the tapes. I was like a sponge. I needed help, and this little gal from Fenton, Missouri, was supplying it. I almost hated to turn her off when I got to the meeting.

The little church that I'd attended on the same piece of property thirty years earlier didn't even resemble what it once was. Now there were two two-story buildings. There were only two cars in the parking lot when I pulled in, and for a while I thought that I was in the wrong place. It wasn't long before the parking lot started filling up, and I followed people up to the second floor. We piled into the small classroom and arranged all of our chairs in a circle. More and more people kept coming, and the circle kept spreading our farther and farther until our backs were all against the wall.

Going alone to a strange place so far away from home where I knew no one was quite a feat for me. I was never a loner. Heck, I couldn't stand to go to Costco by myself. I always cajoled someone into going with me. Now here I was in San Jose at a meeting with twenty strangers. *I must be desperate*, I thought.

The chairperson asked that we go around the room and introduce ourselves. All I had to do was say my name, but I was terrified. It had been a lot easier in a room with only three strangers.

"Hi, my name is Charisse, and I'm a codependent."

The chairperson introduced a heavyset man in his mid-fifties who was the speaker for the evening.

"Hi, my name's Mike, and I'm a codependent. My wife has battled alcoholism for twenty years. She has given up drinking and gone back to it more times than I can count, and each time she starts again she's much worse than the last time. I've learned to separate her from her disease, and I gave up trying to change her. I have given her to God and now she has been sober for two years. I understand that it doesn't mean that she won't start drinking again. I am living one day at a time and appreciating the good

This Can't Be Happening to Me

days. I am a much happier person, and not laying the burden of my happiness on my wife relieves her of a ton of pressure. I think she might make it this time, but even if she starts drinking again, I know that I will be okay."

I cried the entire time he spoke.

After the speaker was finished, people had the opportunity to share if they felt like it. Living in a crazy world with your misery can convince you that no one else has any idea what you are going through. Sitting there listening to story after story about other people dealing with the same things that I was dealing with and feeling the same emotions I was feeling was cathartic. They felt the fear. They knew the shame and the embarrassment. *I'm not crazy. I'm not a bad person. I am just human.*

We held hands and said the Lord's Prayer at the end of the meeting, and I felt more connected to this roomful of strangers than I had felt to anything in quite a long time. It was wonderful. When I said, "I'll see you all on Monday," I meant it. I didn't know how I was going to make it until then.

I got into my car, and when I turned the key in my ignition Joyce began to speak to me immediately. The name of the tape was *Why, God, Why?* She talked about how we go through life ignoring God completely until we feel like we need His help, one more uppercut for the redhead. I deserved it, and I listened to her all the way home. When I got home I found Tommy asleep on the couch with the TV on. I turned off the set and went to our room and put in the codependency video. I finished one and then watched number two.

It was as if a huge lightbulb had been turned on in my head. I was seeing a side of myself that I really didn't care to see. I *was* controlling and manipulative. I *always* had to have my own way. I'd probably drink, too, if I lived with me.

Then she started on perfectionism. *Oh, help me, Jesus; this is going to be rough.* I was a crazy woman when it came to wanting everything done a certain way. My way was the right way, and there was no wiggle room. I had to have the bar set up just so, with everything in its proper place, the way it worked best for me. No one else's opinions mattered to me. Joyce said perfectionists make everyone around them miserable. She said, "No one and nothing is ever perfect, so get over it and lighten up."

She finished with perfectionism and moved on to workaholics. Was there anything that I wasn't going to get raked over the coals about? The bar became my life as soon as I bought it. I put it before everything. Working for myself gave me more pleasure than I had ever imagined. I remembered when Tommy begged me to take a day off. "I will know when it's time to take a day off," I told him. It was four months before I took a day off, and I worried the entire time about what was going on at the bar without me.

My dream became my obsession. It was two years before I started taking two days off in a row, and that was only if there wasn't a football game, birthday party, or dart tournament to attend to. I always found a reason to be at the bar. My husband played second fiddle in my life for a very long time.

Tommy's disease quickly became my excuse for neglecting him and our marriage. After all, it wasn't my fault he was an alcoholic. I was the one who worked and paid the bills. Tommy drank from the time he woke up until he passed out at night. I'd thought about cutting back on my drinking for the sake of our marriage, but in my eyes he was the one with the problem, and I didn't see any reason that I should have to quit. My life was all about me. My dysfunctional past had turned me into the person I had become, and now I had to decide whether I wanted to stay that way at the cost of my marriage.

TRYING TO FIND MY BALANCE

Our strange arrangement of Tommy staying on the couch and avoiding me like the plague went on for about ten days. I tried to talk to him, but he wasn't interested, and I'd heard through the grapevine that he was hanging out at Whiskey Creek. That added insult to injury. I didn't want him to hang out at Johnny's in my face, but I certainly didn't want him spending my hard-earned money at the Creek. I was stuck in a terrible catch-22.

I continued to go to my Al-Anon meetings as well as therapy, and I listened to Joyce's videos and cassette tapes incessantly. I'd gone online and ordered a bunch of her material. I felt like she knew me and could help me see my way out of my misery.

And miserable I was. I cried all the time. I'd started to lean on God a little, but I was still trying to figure things out for myself. I was trying to improve myself while my alcoholic husband continued to go along like nothing had happened. His life hadn't changed a bit while he turned mine upside down. I finally couldn't take it anymore. He was sitting at the bar at the video game machine one morning and I decided to put an end to the uncertainty. He didn't even look away from the machine when I approached.

"Tommy, how long do you intend to go on like this?"

"Go on like what?"

"Go on like what? I'll tell you what. You told me you didn't want to be married to me anymore, and since then I've been falling apart while you go on with life as usual. You continue to drink yourself into oblivion at my expense, sleep on the couch, and refuse to even talk about where we go from here. I can't take it anymore. I'm losing my mind. I believe that God wants us to stay together, but if you won't even try to deal with our problems, we're doomed."

"I don't know what you want me to do."

"Do something. Go to an AA meeting, get some counseling, just do something!"

"I tried AA before. It didn't work for me. I'll never be good enough for you, and there's no use trying. Our marriage was over a long time ago. You just don't want to admit it."

"So what am I supposed to do?" I said, my temper starting to flare. "Continue to pay all of our bills and pay for your booze while you drink yourself to death? Put a roof over your head and gas in your truck while you rip my heart out? I never know whether you're going to stop coming home. You sleep on the couch while I cry all night. It's not fair. It has to stop."

"I have a small job coming up at a place that used to be a convalescent home. The people said I could stay there while I do the work. I'll try to get out of the house in the next couple of days," he said emotionlessly.

I ran to my office, grabbed my purse and keys, and drove home a basket case. Tommy's matter-of-fact attitude and lack of feelings ripped me to the core. It was true: He didn't love me anymore; that was obvious. I could barely see the road through my tears, and I wailed so loudly when I got home that I'm surprised the neighbors didn't call the police. I was in so much pain that I literally thought I would die from it. How could he be so cold?

The more I thought about how badly he was treating me, the madder I got. The madder I got, the less pain I felt—and that was good thing. I resolved to see an attorney the next day. If he thought he was going to live off of me forever, he was wrong. It was about time he took care of himself. And where would he get the

Trying to Find My Balance

money to do that? I didn't care. If he was finished, I was finished, too. If a divorce was what he wanted, I'd see to it that he got one.

* * *

I cried myself to sleep again and woke up at six a.m. and went to the kitchen. Tommy was asleep on the couch. I stood and stared at him for a while. I needed to stay mad, but he looked so pitiful. The living room smelled like old socks and old booze, which brought back my resolve. I decided to sneak out for a walk. When I got back I'd inform him of my plans. I took a brisk forty-minute walk, and when I returned home Tommy was coming out of the bathroom.

"I've been thinking about what you said," I told him. "If we are truly finished we should probably start divorce proceedings. If you get arrested or hurt someone while driving around drunk, you could cost me everything that I have worked so hard for, and I can't take that chance."

"Fine, you have a point. Do what you need to do."

"You're the one who wants a divorce, and now I've got to handle that, too?"

"I wouldn't know where to start, and I'm not the one with the checkbook. Divorces aren't free, you know."

"Do you plan on finding another place to live, or are you going to continue staying here and torturing me?"

"I'll move out today, but I'll have to leave most of my stuff here. The place I'll be staying is only temporary. I'll take some clothes for now, but that will be all."

"Great, and I'll get to work on starting the divorce proceedings."

I was livid. Once again I was left holding the bag. I stormed out of the room and slammed the door to our bedroom so hard that I hurt my shoulder. I jumped in the shower to prepare for work and my search for an attorney.

* * *

I got to Johnny's and knocked out all of my book work as quickly as possible so I could get to work on the attorney situation.

Miracles and Grace in an Unlikely Place

I had no clue where to start. I could have asked John O'Brien, but he had known both Tommy and me since I bought the bar, and it felt a little too close to home. I knew a prominent businesswoman in town, and I figured she would know of a good attorney. My business colleague was sorry to hear about my situation, but was familiar with Tommy's drinking problem, and she had just the guy for me.

I called the attorney's office and he managed to squeeze me in that day at four o'clock. I could still make my therapist appointment first, so it would work out well. When I told Dr. Sullivan that I was seeing a divorce lawyer, he seemed pleased. He hadn't given our marriage a snowball's chance in hell of making it anyway. After our meeting I headed back to Hollister to meet with the attorney.

* * *

Mr. Duran's office had leather chairs and dark wood furniture. He was tall and dressed in a nice suit with cowboy boots. Could I expect anything else in Hollister? He had a firm handshake and a barracuda demeanor. I felt like he could surely look out for my best interests.

We sat down and I filled him in on my situation. He told me his normal retainer was $2,500. My mouth hit the floor. After he spelled out my situation based on California's community property statutes, I asked why the heck I would give him $2,500 so that my husband could take half of everything I owned. He told me that a paralegal was probably my best bet.

I left the office completely deflated. I could understand Tommy getting half of our house, but the bar was quite another story. I used my inheritance for the down payment, and I was the one who'd worked it all these years while my husband drank up the profits. There was no way that I would give him half of what I'd worked so hard for. I couldn't even imagine him asking for half. He wasn't that cold.

That was a bad assumption on my part. I found a paralegal and explained to Tommy that for $400 she would file our divorce papers for us once we decided how we were going to divide up our

Trying to Find My Balance

property. In the meantime we needed to file for a legal separation, relieving me of any financial responsibilities for bills he continued to rack up. I'd paid off numerous charge cards in the past that he very irresponsibly ran through the roof, and I was through with that. I made an appointment for the following week and asked Tommy to meet me there.

While I was in self-preservation mode I cried a lot less, at least during the day. Nights were horrible. The first night that Tommy didn't come home was excruciating. Even though we hadn't been sleeping together, knowing that he was in the house brought me some comfort. I thought I would lose my mind with conflicting feelings. I wanted to choke him, but I missed his presence. It made no sense at all. I told myself that if he wanted to move on, I'd move on, too.

I knew if he took half of everything that I had worked so hard for, I could build myself back up again. He would most certainly drink away his half and wind up with nothing. The thought should have brought me pleasure, but instead it broke my heart. I couldn't stand thinking about him all used up with nothing in his life. Still, I certainly didn't want to think about him sharing his half with someone else. Holy crap, I needed help. I was a basket case.

* * *

I filled my days with Al-Anon meetings, Joyce Meyer books and tapes, self-help books, and my Bible. I read incessantly and never turned on the TV or the radio. Something inside of me knew that there was a lesson to be learned that would make me a better person in the end. I decided to follow the advice dished out at my meetings and just take one day at a time.

* * *

The day Tommy met me at the paralegal's office, I matched his cold demeanor with one of my own. Ms. Garrett's office was on the bottom floor of a business complex on San Benito Street. She was pleasant and unbiased and gave us the facts. She explained once again California's community property laws and said that the process was pretty straightforward. When she said, "Each of you gets half of everything," Tommy had a smug look on his face.

"I read somewhere that an inheritance does not fall under those rules," I told her. "I bought Johnny's with my inheritance, so wouldn't that make it exempt?"

"If you have proof of the inheritance, that amount would be deducted from the sale of the bar or the bar's appraised value, but the rest would be split down the middle," she said.

"But he knows that it's been all of my hard work that made the bar what it is," I said, as if Tommy weren't sitting right next to me.

"You heard the lady," Tommy said. "It's California law."

"But it's not right," I yelped.

"I've done plenty in that bar over the years. You just never gave me any credit for it. Who do you think remodeled it, and fixes stuff every time something breaks?"

"Are you kidding me? You spent maybe three months off and on remodeling the place, and you pretty much stopped fixing anything without a knock-down, drag-out fight four years ago. I've worked my ass off for six years while you drink up half the profits. You are delusional, pal."

"I'm sorry, Charisse," Ms. Garrett said. "Tom has the law on his side. Why don't we just file for the separation for now and you two can take these papers home and look them over. We'll deal with the actual divorce after you've had some time to discuss more of the details."

We signed the paperwork, took our copies, and headed for the door. When we got into the parking lot I glared at Tommy and said, "If you think you're going to get away with half of everything, you're crazy."

"The law is the law," he said.

I screeched out of the parking lot and went to the bar for a stiff drink. The usual clan was there and sympathetically listened to me rave on, but they all agreed that I was screwed. I couldn't believe that Tommy would do that to me. He wasn't acting anything like the man I married. It was as if a crazy alien had taken over his body. I was sure that when he calmed down he would see how unreasonable he was being.

Trying to Find My Balance

I would have thrown back a few cocktails but I had my Alanon meeting in San Jose to go to and I wasn't about to go there loopy. I hadn't been able to speak at the meetings because I cried through all of them but I felt like I might be able to share a little this evening. I decided to leave early and go to Aunt Joannie's so I wouldn't be tempted to drink anymore.

I put on Joyce for my ride to San Jose, and by the time I got to Joannie's house I was back to being a puddle again. Joyce said that God wasn't obligated to get you out of a situation that He never told you to get into. She said we rush in with our own plans and don't ask God what He thinks about them, and then when they don't work out we expect Him to bail us out. I heard God's voice again saying: *You were married to an alcoholic and you bought a bar. What did you expect?* I didn't want to be accountable for that choice. I wanted to blame everything on Tommy, the way I had been doing for years.

Joannie went with me to the meeting, and I was glad for the company. Not so coincidentally, I'm sure, the theme of the evening was accountability. The chairperson took responsibility for her part in her husband's demise, which led to everyone who shared that night doing the same. God saw to it that I was forced into seeing my culpability in our mess. It was a very painful ordeal, and once again I cried through the entire meeting. I got more hugs when I left that night than I ever had before. Everyone let me know that they were praying for me, which I deeply appreciated. I passed on Joannie's offer to treat me to pie at Marie Callender's. I just wanted to get home.

I put Joyce's tape in the player, but found that I couldn't listen to it. I felt like I needed some time alone with God. I turned off the cassette player and started praying out loud. "Dear God, please forgive me. I want to accept responsibility for my part in the big mess I've made of my life. I knew Tommy was an alcoholic, but I followed my dream. I put my wishes before our marriage. I am a selfish bitch. Sorry, God. I have demeaned my husband for so long that he probably doesn't have an ounce of self-esteem left. I am so sorry, Lord. Please forgive me. Help my husband to forgive me. Please don't let me lose him, God. Please save our marriage."

I sobbed for most of the drive home, and vacillated between feeling sorry for myself and being angry at myself for getting into such a mess. "But, God," I pleaded, "everything came together so well just at the right time. I believed it was the right thing to do. Is it possible that I was so completely wrong?"

When I got home I went right to bed and cried myself to sleep again. I woke up at three a.m. and I had a serious come-to-Jesus meeting. If I wanted things to change, I knew it would have to start with me.

"Okay, God, you know my heart," I prayed. "You know I love my husband and I don't want a divorce. I want you to show me my part in this mess. I want you to show me the person my husband sees. Reveal me to me. Show me my defects so that I can be the person that you want me to be. You're the potter and I'm the clay, Lord. Help me, please, I beg of you. Save my marriage."

Take it from me, if you don't want to know the truth from God, do not ask Him to show it to you. God showed me more of myself than I ever wanted to see. The visions that He put before me brought me more shame than I ever thought possible. The loving, kind, and giving person I considered myself to be was not the person who ran through my memory banks now. He opened my eyes to the fact that I always had to have my own way. I turned a deaf ear to other people's needs if they in any way interfered with mine. I insulted and demeaned my husband several times a day. I stepped all over people who got in my way. I was a selfish, controlling bitch, plain and simple.

I repented and asked for forgiveness. I asked God to change me, not my husband. I thanked Him for loving such a flawed and screwed-up individual. Slowly a peace came over me like I had never known. I heard God speaking to my heart: *Your marriage will be saved. I love you and I forgive you, and one day Tommy will, too. Just leave him to Me.*

My tears of sadness and regret turned into tears of joy, and I believed what God said with all of my heart. When I fell asleep again I had the best sleep that I had had in as long as I could remember.

LIGHT AT THE END OF THE TUNNEL

I woke the next morning feeling refreshed, and popped out of bed and got right into my exercise tape. When I finished it I headed out for my walk. Jeannie was dealing with very big problems of her own and couldn't walk with me, so I called my mom on my cell phone. I just had to tell someone what God had spoken to me.

"Hi, Mom, it's me," I said when she answered the phone.

"You sound chipper today. You must be feeling better."

"You have no idea, Mom. I went to the best Al-Anon meeting last night."

"You did? What made it such a great meeting?"

"Accountability. Everyone talked about the part they played in their loved one's sickness. It went right along with what Joyce was saying on the tape I listened to on the way to San Jose. I've been so busy blaming Tommy for everything that I haven't taken a personal inventory of myself and my actions. God revealed some things to me last night. And He forgave me, Mom. I know what true repentance feels like, and it is wonderful. The big news is that He told me my marriage would be saved if I leave Tommy in His capable hands."

"I'm happy for you. I've been praying for you every day."

"Well, it paid off, Mom. I haven't felt this good in a very long time. It's a beautiful day. I can't wait to call my honey later and talk to him."

"Charisse, remember, God spoke to you, not him. Things will not miraculously change overnight. He's going to need some time."

"I know, Mom. Especially after the big fight we had at the paralegal's office."

I told my mother about the screaming match in the paralegal's parking lot and filled her in on what I'd learned about Tommy getting half of everything. She didn't think it was fair either, but I told her, "Fair or not, it is the law. But it doesn't matter, Mom, because we're not getting a divorce. God said so, and if He be for me, who can be against me?"

"I'm just happy you're feeling better."

"I feel like a thousand-pound weight has been lifted off of my shoulders. I'm about home now, so I'm going to let you go, Mom. I'll keep you informed." I hung up and skipped up my driveway.

* * *

Later that day I called Tommy to see whether he would come to dinner the following night. I'd arranged to go to a spa retreat in a week, and he was going to take care of the cats. I told him we should get together to talk about the arrangements, and I figured he could use a home-cooked meal. He apprehensively said yes; he wanted to eat a nice dinner, but I'm sure the serene tone of my voice was unsettling. I went from a screaming lunatic one day to a composed gal that wanted to make him dinner the next.

* * *

I was so excited the following day that I could hardly contain myself. I went to Johnny's to take care of book work, and many people told me how much better I looked. "I feel much better," I told them without explanation. I didn't think they would understand if I shared my revelation. I stopped at the grocery store on the way home, cleaned the house, and prepared a wonderful meal that included a steak for me and salmon for Tommy. I hate fish and he loves it. He very seldom got to eat it, so I thought I'd surprise him. When Tommy knocked on the door at five thirty I swung it open with a big smile on my face.

"I wasn't sure what to do," he said. "I still have my key, but I felt funny using it."

"No worries. Come on in. I waited to put your salmon on until you got here. I know how you hate overcooked fish."

"What made you decide to fix salmon? You hate fish."

"I got a steak for myself. I know you haven't been eating right, and I figured some fish would be good for you."

"Okay," Tommy said. He looked like he was expecting the *Candid Camera* guys to pop out from somewhere. "This is nice and all, but what the heck is going on here?"

"Well, I was going to ease into that, but since you brought it up I'll get right to it. You know that I've been going to Al-Anon. I went to a meeting last night and the speaker talked about owning up to our part of the problems because of our codependency. It really opened my eyes. Joyce Meyer—that's the lady I told you I've been listening to a lot lately—spoke on the same subject, and I knew that God was trying to tell me something. I actually had a pretty good conversation with Him last night, and He told me that we're going to stay together."

"Who said we're going to stay together?"

"God."

"You talked to God and you think He told you that we're going to stay together?"

"No, I know He told me that we're going to stay together."

"Didn't we just file our separation papers and start the divorce proceedings?"

"We filed for a legal separation. I was in protection mode. If you hurt someone while driving around drunk I will have to pay the price, because we could lose everything. I also know how you are with the Visa card. I've paid off thousands of dollars of debt, and you put us right back in the hole every time. I was just looking out for myself. I was hurt and scared, but I haven't filed the actual divorce papers yet."

"Excuse me if I'm a little confused. Were you not in the parking lot having a screaming match with me just days ago?"

"I was freaked out. You started saying all that stuff about getting half of everything, and I was angry. I don't care what California law says; we both know that would not have been fair. If it weren't for my inheritance and hard work there would be no Johnny's."

"So here we go again with 'your bar.'"

"None of that stuff matters now. Things are going to be different; I promise you. Just give me a chance. Let's have a nice dinner and go over the days I'll be gone next week. You'll be staying here with the babies, right?"

"Yeah, I guess."

"Cool. Let's eat."

We talked about my trip and enjoyed a meal together. When Tommy left after dinner, I knew his head was spinning. I'd done a complete one-eighty in two days' time, and I knew I'd confused the heck out of him. I was glad that I'd only given Ms. Garrett $95 to file the separation papers, because she wasn't getting any more of my money.

HEALING FOR MY MIND, BODY, AND SPIRIT

I left for the Green Valley Spa in Saint George, Utah, for a five-night stay on February 12, 2002. My friend Lys had gone there when she was going through a rough patch, and she said it brought her back to life. It was very expensive, and I didn't usually spend that kind of money on myself, but I had savings, and I figured I'd earned it. Tommy agreed to take me to the airport, and I'm quite sure he was baffled by me. It seemed like he was always waiting for the other shoe to drop. With a firm resolve to save our marriage, I remained pleasant and hopeful, and he wasn't sure what to make of me.

"You have everything you need?" he asked as I brought my bags to the front door.

"Yep, I'm ready to go. I'm going to miss my babies, but I know their dad will take good care of them."

When Tommy dropped me off in the Southwest departure area, I kissed his cheek and thanked him before heading to the skycap.

He still had a suspicious look on his face when I walked away. The poor man did not know what to make of his crazy redhead.

* * *

I arrived at the Green Valley Spa pretty late in the afternoon and was greeted by a very hospitable lady. She showed me where my room was on the map and pointed out all of the resort's amenities, including the pool, labyrinth, gym, dining hall, and spa. She told me that I would have time to relax in my room before joining everyone for dinner, where we were expected to wear the pajamas that were provided. Pajamas to dinner, seriously? She explained that the goal of Green Valley was to destress its guests, and that wearing pajamas to dinner encouraged guests to relax.

"I think I'm going to like this place," I told her.

The spa was just what the doctor ordered. Everything was geared toward health, and all of the meals were included. Snacks were always available, and they included string cheese, hard-boiled eggs, apples, oranges, yogurt, and trail mix. Exercise classes were offered all day long, with everything from yoga to spinning. Hikes were arranged at every level of endurance, from beginner to advanced. There were classes in meditation and journaling, and speakers on the subjects rounded out the schedule.

I entered my room and it was filled with the scent of lilacs and chamomile. In the middle of the room was a plush queen-size bed that beckoned me like a fluffy cloud. I had to jump in to see whether it felt as good as it looked, and I wasn't disappointed. The pillow-soft bed, sheets, and comforter wrapped around me like a sumptuous cocoon.

There was a nice sitting area to the right of the bed that led out to a little patio, where I had a view of the pool. The bathroom to the left had a huge jetted tub with an assortment of scented bath bubbles. The large vanity was adorned with candles and assorted face and body creams, as well as salt scrubs and loofas. The robe that hung behind the door was so luxurious and comfortable that I hated to put the pajamas on underneath it. They were made of a cotton blend and were cozy and warm. The slippers that matched were just as comfortable. I had never dreamed of being treated to such luxury in my life. I had to fight the urge to feel guilty. I told myself repeatedly, "You deserve this."

As I dressed for dinner in my pajamas, I pinched myself to be sure that I wasn't dreaming. Lys said Green Valley was nice, but she never got close to describing this. I headed to the dining hall and was escorted to a table where three people were already seated. All of the tables accommodated six people, and we were encouraged to get to know our tablemates. I met a wonderful couple who had been to Saint George three times, and they schooled me in how to get the most from the retreat.

Included in my stay were two spa treatments, and there was a bevy of them to choose from. Reflexology, hydrotherapy, detox and cleansing scrubs, deep-tissue massages, as well as facials, pedicures, and manicures were among my choices. My New York friend told me to book my treatments for about eight o'clock at night so I could go to bed totally relaxed and let all of the wonderful creams and lotions soak into my skin all night long. I took her advice and scheduled a treatment for my second night at the retreat. I spent my first full day getting the lay of the land and joined in on tai chi, yoga, and low-impact aerobics classes, after which I enjoyed the pool and hot tub. I couldn't believe how warm it was in Utah in February. I truly felt like God had taken care of everything, including the weather, just for me.

The meals were fiber-rich, low-carb, and low-calorie, as well as organic. They were prepared by four-star chefs, but it was a bit much for this bona fide, country, meat-and-potatoes girl. I found myself relishing the snacks provided. After dinner I went to my room and read for a while before heading out for my treatment.

The Rapunzel, as it was so aptly named, was performed outside, and included a shampoo with the most aromatic stuff I've ever had on my head. The table I stretched out on looked similar to a massage table, but the headpiece was smaller, giving my treatment specialist room to work. My head in the cradle, warm, soothing water was poured over it. The shampoo was slowly massaged into my hair, and when the lather was rinsed out an equally aromatic conditioner was applied. There is no describing the scalp massage that went along with the treatment. It was one of the most pleasurable experiences I'd ever had.

A salt scrub was applied to my neck, chest, and shoulders, and when it was rinsed off wonderful lotions and emollients were massaged in. When the therapist was finished with my treatment, she wrapped my head in a big warm towel. I floated back to my room, where I found my bed turned down, there was glorious harp music playing on the CD player, and the smell of lilacs filled the room. "Thank you, Jesus," I crooned. "I don't deserve this."

I took off my robe and crawled under the cushy comforter of my cloud bed, and as I snuggled in I began weeping. I felt so unworthy and undeserving. The crazy-bitch bar owner who'd stomped all over her husband's manhood for years, as well as bulldozing her way across quite a few well-meaning friends and employees, did not deserve this fantastic treatment. There could not have been a better setting to have a talk with God. I should really say that He had a talk with me.

As I lay there crying and feeling like the world's biggest jerk, I heard God's still, small voice: *It is time for you to forgive yourself.*

"But, God, I've been so selfish," I told Him. Again I heard His words: *It's time for you to forgive yourself.*

Then I remembered something that Joyce Meyer said: "Hurting people hurt people." I was overwhelmed by God's grace. I knew that He understood that I had become a product of the things that I had been through. I knew that when I came out on the other side a better person, He could use me to help others. I saw God's purpose for my life, and I could not wait to make Him proud. I knew I had it in me. I was a changed person, and I knew that my husband would see that and want me back. God was very clear that it would be in His timing, but I was in it for the long haul. I called Tommy to say good night and check on the cats.

"How's it going?" I asked.

"It's going."

"Listen, honey, I've had some serious God time today, and I just want to tell you how sorry I am for the way that I treated you for years. I didn't realize what I was doing to you, and I regret my behavior very much. I hope you can forgive me."

"Why are you apologizing to me? I'm the drunk. I don't know what this is all about, but no apologies necessary, okay?"

"No, it's not okay. I beat you up verbally on a pretty regular basis. I disrespected you in front of customers and it added to their disrespect for you, and I am sorry. I have changed and things will change. I only hope that you'll give me another chance."

"Okay, now you're starting to freak me out. Are you okay?"

"I am absolutely wonderful, honey. As a matter of fact, I couldn't be better. This place is so awesome I can't even describe it. The people are great, and I've never been pampered like this in my life."

"That's good," he said. There was tenderness in his voice that I hadn't heard in quite some time, and after I hung up I thanked Jesus repeatedly. I was still thanking Him when I finally dozed off.

* * *

I was all about new beginnings, and the timing couldn't have been better to do some out-of-the-ordinary things. I signed up for a 4.7-mile fitness hike on my second day that took us through the Padre Canyon. The promised trek through red rock, sand dunes, and caverns, and around ponds and streams was filled with exhilarating views. I saw God's splendor like never before, up close and personal, and I'd never felt closer to him. How could anyone see this and not believe in God? I wondered. The next day I did the Green Valley Challenge, which consisted of a five-mile hike including rock climbing, rappelling three hundred and twenty-five feet down the face of a mountain, and flying down a zip line across a two-hundred-foot canyon. It was one of the scariest and most exhilarating things I had done in my life. After five days of exercise, meditation, relaxation, and wonderful one-on-one God time, I left Utah a stronger and more determined woman than I thought I could ever be. I was ready to take on the world.

* * *

Miracles and Grace in an Unlikely Place

If I wasn't freaking Tommy out enough when he dropped me off at the airport, I'm sure he was totally bewildered when he brought me home from Saint George. I called him from the spa every day and told him that I loved him and was praying for us, and even though I'd mentioned many times that I was a changed person, Ms. Bubbles threw him for a loop.

He brought my luggage into the house and I asked if he'd like to stay for a while. He declined the offer, and I kissed him on the cheek as he turned to leave. As I watched him drive off I became incredibly blue. I knew that he needed time, but I wanted him to move back home right away. I'd never seen the place he moved into, and to this day I have no idea how bad it was. I don't think it could have been any worse than what I pictured in my mind. I imagined a bunch of small rooms down long corridors, with dirty cots and no electricity. It was dark, cold, and dank, and it was no place for the love of my life to be living. When I crawled in bed and pictured him there I cried myself to sleep for the first time in four days, a new record since Tommy had told me we were through.

PRAYING AND BELIEVING

We were separated for three months, and I begged God every night to bring my honey home. A couple of days after my retreat I had Tommy over for dinner, and I told him that I wanted him to move back in. I told him that I didn't care if he stayed on the couch; I just couldn't stand thinking of him in that awful place. He made light of it and told me that it wasn't that bad.

Finally, one night when he came to the house for dinner Tommy told me that he had been thinking a lot about it and that he wanted to move back home.

"I don't do things fast the way that you do," he told me. "I'm going to stay on the couch for a while, because I need to go slowly and figure out how I feel about all of this. If you're okay with that, I'll move back in."

"That's fine with me, honey. You take all the time you need. I'll just be glad you're home again."

* * *

Miracles and Grace in an Unlikely Place

His first night back home we had dinner together and watched TV while holding hands. At ten o'clock I kissed Tommy on the forehead and told him that I would let him get some sleep. I hadn't seen him stay awake past ten o'clock in a long time, and I wanted him to feel comfortable. When I crawled into our bed alone again I thanked God that my husband was home, even if he wasn't in our bed. "Your timing, not mine, Lord," I said. I cried tears of relief because I didn't have to picture him in that awful place.

* * *

I continued to grow spiritually through reading my Bible and listening to my Joyce Meyer tapes, but I knew I needed to find a church family. My good friend Heather invited me to join her at Rolling Hills Church one Sunday. The people were warm and friendly, and once I heard Pastor Henry speak I knew I was in the right place. Having the wonderful friends I met there as my prayer partners gave me the resolve and strength I needed to hang in there. I had no idea how much I was going to need to lean on them.

* * *

Tommy slept on the couch for about three weeks before making his way back into our bedroom. One evening when I kissed him good night as usual, he said, "I thought I would sleep in our bed tonight." I was so happy I thought my heart would burst.

"Really," I said. "That would be great."

"I still need to go slowly," he said. "I don't want you to be disappointed."

"Just having you next to me will be wonderful."

We turned off the lights and got undressed and crawled into bed like two young lovers who had never been together before. Tommy wrapped his arms around me, and tears started rolling down my cheeks. I willed them to stop, because I didn't want to scare him off. I cringed as one of them dripped onto his hand, but instead of being bothered, he rolled me over, wiped the tears from my face, and kissed me tenderly. We made love for the first time in what seemed like an eternity, and it was incredible. As hard as I tried, the tears of joy would not stop flowing. Damn, I was tired of crying.

THE ONLY WAY OUT IS TO GO THROUGH

TRYING TO DO IT GOD'S WAY— NO ONE SAID IT WAS GOING TO BE EASY

For about six months life was beautiful. I was thrilled to have my husband back. People would ask, "Is he still drinking?" "Yes, he is," I would say, "but not nearly as much." Tommy did try hard to cut back, but an alcoholic is an alcoholic is an alcoholic.

God's hand in our lives was evident, and I witnessed small miracles almost daily. This reinforced my belief that since I was doing what He asked me to do—be more loving and understanding, be less combative, and pray about everything—He would make my husband quit drinking quickly. This was not, however, his plan.

Eventually Tommy fell back into the old habit of consuming two fifths of booze a day, and I fell back into my old habit of trying to get him to quit drinking, for us. His jobs were few and far between. As hard as I tried not to turn back into the nagging wife, I couldn't seem to keep my mouth shut. I was miserable once again, because I never seemed to see my husband sober. The smell of Jack Daniel's oozed from his pores. I felt cheated. I'd worked so hard to save our marriage. I was a changed person in so many ways. I

Trying to Do It God's Way— No One Said It Was Going to Be Easy

prayed daily that Tommy would quit drinking. He had many medical issues and was miserable all the time.

He had a liver biopsy, and I went to his follow-up appointment with him, because I was sure that he wasn't telling me everything the doctor said. His doctor told him that 80 percent of his health issues were related to alcohol, but he didn't tell him to stop drinking. I was angry. I wanted him to tell Tommy to quit drinking or die. When I told the doctor as much, he said, "You're asking me to wash your dog even though you know he's going to bite me." His analogy stunned me, but he made a good point. He knew that telling Tommy to stop would not make him do it.

* * *

I'd started going to Joyce Meyer conferences when they were close, and even to her women's conference in Saint Louis, Missouri, and I read many of her books. Her type A, choleric personality was a lot like mine, and I related to her well. It was at one of those conferences that she finally got through my head what God had been trying to tell me all along: I needed to let go and let God. I was giving lip service to leaving Tommy in His hands, but still trying to change him myself. I needed to shut my mouth when I wanted to tell him that he was killing himself and drinking us broke. I needed to stop complaining about him, even to my best friend. I needed to start professing with my mouth that my husband would quit drinking the same way I professed and believed that our marriage would be saved. I came home from Saint Louis determined to do what God asked of me.

* * *

The tests began right away. The Visa bill with many Rite Aid charges for Jack Daniel's and vodka came. Tommy and a friend were out in his shop, ripped and playing with power tools. I told Tommy about something that needed to be fixed and he told me that he'd get to it, if he could remember. And the stench of his breath about killed me. It filled whatever room he was in. At night

Miracles and Grace in an Unlikely Place

I hung my head off of the side of our bed so that I could breathe. When I came home from work, if he was in a cantankerous mood I went straight to our room. If he said something that set me off, I ran and put my face in my pillow and screamed at the top of my lungs instead of snapping back at him. As well as dealing with Tommy's problems I was trying to handle issues at the bar in a more Christian fashion. It wasn't easy, especially where rallies were concerned.

I TOLD YOU NOT TO
MAKE THEM ANGRY

Rallies presented a ton of difficulties on a regular basis. Fighting the city council to keep them alive was standard practice, with the exception of 1999 through 2005, when the Independence Rally Committee had an ongoing contract. It made planning for it a little easier, but the biggest hurdle was finding trustworthy employees. The first official rally in 1997 taught me that I needed a lot more cash registers and a lot more accountability. Every rally people who promised they were going to work would flake on me without sufficient notice. Sometimes people just didn't show up. No apologies or even a phone call.

Year after year, in hopes of making things go more smoothly, I deciphered ways of doing things differently, but regardless, new trials arose. A beer cooler would die, or my computer would crash. The ice machine would go on the fritz, or the walk-in cooler would quit. There was always so much to do, and I didn't get much help from Tommy. It incensed me that he would complain when I asked him to make sure that I had proper lighting on the patio when I was doing four hundred other things to make our rally weekend a success. He snapped at me and became such an ass that I got customers to help me out as much as possible so that I didn't need to ask him to do anything. If I ran out of something and asked him to make a trip to Costco, you'd think I'd asked him to fly to the moon, not drive to Gilroy.

In 2002, when he informed me that his friends in Shasta wanted him to go to their house for the Fourth of July weekend, I said, "Be free; go and have a good time." It was easier on me in the long run, because I didn't have to listen to him snivel and complain.

* * *

The entire month of June right through the rally was always intense for me. Since something happened to add to my stress level before the rally every year, I began dreading whatever it was going to be before it even happened. In hindsight I think I brought things on myself with my lousy mind-set. My big mouth may have had a little something to do with the issues with the Hollister Police Department. I repeatedly told the city council and the chief himself that the actions he took during the rally were out of line and completely unnecessary.

* * *

On Friday night of the 2002 rally, at ten p.m. we were absolutely slammed when two ABC officers came in and asked Kat to step outside. I was livid and wanted an explanation. Apparently two underage girls they picked up drunk told them that Kat had served them at Johnny's. I knew that it was a bogus claim for two reasons: Number one, I had long ago replaced the aforementioned security company with some wonderful Clampers who had my back at all costs and would never have allowed minors into the bar in the first place. During the rally we carded everyone, no matter how old, and didn't let them in the building without an ID. Number two, Kat would card my mother if she thought she looked underage, despite having bouncers in place. They were picking on

I Told You Not to Make Them Angry

the wrong girl. Kat was terrified. The officers said they were taking her to be booked, and I can still see the horror on her face to this day. I was like a mother watching her child being carted off. I told the cops that I was going with her, and they said it was out of the question. I was beside myself, but had to pull it together and help behind the bar while waiting to hear from my petrified little bartender.

At around eleven thirty I saw Kat in the kitchen and dropped everything to talk to her.

"Kat, what happened? How are you?"

The poor girl was shaking. "The cops put me in a room with one-way glass and asked the girls on the other side whether I was the one who served them. They both said that I was. I never even got to face my accusers. The cops took the girls' word for it without giving me the opportunity to defend myself. I'm sure that I refused to serve them before for lack of an ID and they had an ax to grind. The cops wrote me a citation and let me go."

She handed me the ticket and her hand was shaking.

"Maybe you should go home."

"I'm not letting those jerks ruin my entire evening. I'm going back to work."

"Don't worry, Kat, because I'm going to hire an attorney and prove that the entire incident was based on harassment."

I gave a well-known attorney a $1,500 retainer and the DA never pressed charges. I got most of the money back but regardless, it cost me $350 for the attorney to write a letter and handle one telephone call.

* * *

In 2004, two days before the rally, a reliable source said he heard through the grapevine that a mother had called the ABC office and complained that her seventeen-year-old son had been served twice at Johnny's. Once again I was sure it was bogus. Because I am a take-the-bull-by-the-horns individual, I called the Salinas Alcoholic Beverage Control office and asked to speak with the officer in charge. When I asked Ms. Sanchez about the rumor, she told me that she hadn't heard anything like that, but that she had seen Johnny's name go across her desk. She put me on hold while she looked for the note. After about five minutes she came back on the line and asked, "Do you have a portables bar on your patio there at Johnny's?"

"Why, yes, I do. I use it every year for the Fourth of July weekend," I replied.

"We don't have record of a license here for that bar."

"I've used the bar for nine years, and no one has ever mentioned that it required one," I told her.

"Oh, yes, I'm afraid it does, and until you get one I would advise you not to use the bar."

I inquired about how to get one, incensed because I was sure it was just another form of harassment. Now, only days before the rally, I had to deal with this very serious issue. Without my patio bar, I would lose thousands of dollars in business.

Ms. Sanchez instructed me to draw up a diagram with the dimensions of the bar and its placement on the patio and bring it to her office, along with a check. I almost choked when she told me the cost, but I had no choice but to comply. Luckily, when I explained the situation to Tommy, he came to the bar right away without complaint, drew up the map, and took it and the check to Salinas. I told him to ask for Ms. Sanchez, and to hurry, because she was going to lunch at noon.

"Just because I'm paranoid doesn't mean they aren't after me," is one of Tommy's favorite sayings, and in this case I believed it was true. I also believed that God's divine intervention was at play again, because if I hadn't called the ABC about the false rumor, I wouldn't have found out about the license, and the cops would certainly have closed down my patio bar in the middle of the rally. It would have been a terrible blow financially.

Tommy called me from the Salinas office about forty minutes later. "I got here and they said there are papers that you need to sign."

"That's crazy; I told Ms. Sanchez I was sending you, and she never said anything about me needing to sign papers."

"They say if you don't come here and sign them, they need to be notarized."

I Told You Not to Make Them Angry

"I can't believe this. I'm doing fifty things to prepare for the rally; I can't leave the bar now. Come back with the forms and I'll take them to the bank and get them notarized."

Before Tommy left the ABC office he asked whether he should leave the check and was told that he should bring it back with him when he brought back the paperwork. Tommy was still drinking at this time. The entire ordeal was pushing him over the edge.

I was busy at the bar arranging the patio for the Porta Potti delivery and putting away the buttload of groceries that were being delivered. I called the bank and made sure that a notary would be available. Irene heard the panic in my voice, was very sympathetic, and said she would hold off on going to lunch to make sure we got the paperwork handled. When Tommy arrived we ran to the bank and got the papers notarized. Then he rushed back to Salinas. Forty minutes later he called me and he was very close to going postal. When he got back to the ABC office and handed in the paperwork and the check, the secretary told him that she couldn't accept a check.

"What the hell do you mean, they can't take a check?" They've been taking my checks for nine years, and now my check isn't good enough?" I screamed.

"Don't yell at me," Tommy screeched back. "I'm just telling you what they said. I asked her to give me the check back so I could try to get cash for it and she wouldn't even give it back. I've never heard of such crap in my life. I'm at Applebee's right now getting a drink, because I wanted to pull the lady over the counter by her neck. I don't remember the last time I was this mad."

"Did you ask to talk to Ms. Sanchez?"

"Yeah, and she's at lunch. I don't know what to do. I'm about to lose it here."

Somehow God blew a little sanity into my ear. I took a deep breath and said, "Okay, honey, I want you to have a drink and some lunch and calm down. I'm going to call the supervisor when she returns from her break and ask her what the darn problem is. She was real nice on the phone, and I'm sure she'll straighten all this out."

"Okay, but if she doesn't fix this I'm done. You'll have to come and deal with it yourself or I'm gonna hurt someone."

"Don't worry, honey. We'll get it straightened out. You just relax and have a nice lunch."

I hung up the phone and prayed that God would help us work things out so that I wouldn't lose my mind. I called the ABC office after one o'clock, when I thought Ms. Sanchez would be back from lunch. I explained that when Tommy came back with the paperwork and the check, the clerk said that they couldn't take a check, which was ludicrous. Ms. Sanchez told me that they had accepted the check and that my husband was on his way home. She also advised me not to open the bar until the license was processed, which could possibly be after the weekend.

* * *

On Thursday night I didn't open the patio bar, but on Friday morning I said the heck with it. I figured I'd show the cops the temporary license when they asked to see it. Despite the fact that no one had ever asked to see a license for the patio bar before, at two o'clock Friday afternoon, when the band of merry officers were making their rounds through the bar, they asked to speak to the owner.

"As you very well know, I am the owner. What can I do for you, Officer?" I said sarcastically. I hated the fact that they pretended that they didn't know who I was.

"Have you got a license for the bar out here?" the officer asked.

"You bet I do, pal," I said as I swung around and headed into the bar to retrieve it. I handed it to the cop and said, "For nine years I've had this bar out here, and no one ever asked to see a license. Isn't it funny that you should ask this year?"

"I guess you were lucky," he said. "And I'd watch your head count. We wouldn't want to have to ask the fire department to close you down for being over capacity."

"Don't you worry; we're watching everything very closely. And if you guys want to suggest that we served a minor, be sure that you know exactly what time it was and where it took place, because I have eleven cameras now that cover every inch of the bar. You're going to have to prove your accusations this time." I turned on my

I Told You Not to Make Them Angry

heel and walked away before I got myself into any further trouble. I was boiling mad.

* * *

Every time I got through another rally I'd pray that the next one would be less stressful. With Tommy spending the weekend with friends in Shasta, we weren't at each other's throats, but I wanted a husband who could help me out during the most stressful times in my life. It just wasn't meant to be.

AM I FINALLY GETTING A BREAK?

I continued to pray that Tommy would quit drinking, but I'd started to doubt that the day would ever come. I had almost given up hope. Then one night I thought my break had finally come. It was actually Tommy's ankle that broke, in three places. We went out for Japanese food for Jeannie's birthday. Tommy was waxed before we even left the bar, and he pounded back sake bombs at the restaurant. I'd been drinking quite a bit, too, and wasn't in the mood to put up with my drunken husband.

I should never have considered letting him drive, but I just wanted him out of my face. I told him to go home, that I would ride back to the bar with our friends Pete and Heather. I was sitting at the bar whining to Jeana about how obnoxious my husband had been at dinner when he came through the back door. I took one look at him and said, "Oh, dear God, help me," and down he went. He caught the tip of his cowboy boot on a bar stool and the stool didn't move. He was lying on the floor and I just ignored him. He was trying to get up when Pete and Heather went to help him, and I heard Heather say, "I don't think you should stand up on that, Tommy; we'd better get that boot off.

Am I Finally Getting a Break?

"Charisse," she said, "this doesn't look good. I think you should get him to the hospital."

I flew off my stool, ready to snatch my husband off the floor, when I saw his ankle. It reminded me of the Joe Theismann leg break of 1985. His ankle was going in a direction that just wasn't right. I have a very weak constitution, and when I saw his ankle I had to lean up against the post to keep from passing out.

"Oh, my God, what have you done?" I said.

"Why don't you pull your car around front, Charisse," Heather said, "and we'll carry him to it so you can get him to the hospital."

"I can't believe this is happening," I said.

I wasn't in any condition to drive, but I didn't feel like I had a choice. I pulled my car up front, and with the help of Pete and Heather and a couple other customers, we managed to get Tommy in the back of my car. We put the seats down so that he could stretch out and not bend his ankle any further. As soon as they closed the door I started in on Tommy.

"You stupid man, I told you to go home. Why didn't you just go home? You were already wasted. Why did you need to come to the bar?"

"I didn't know where you were," he said.

"What do you mean, you didn't know where I was? Where the hell did you think I was? I told you I was riding back to the bar with Pete and Heather. I'd had all I could take of your drunken ass. Now look what you've done. Now I'll have hospital bills to contend with, like you're not stretching me enough. How much more do I have to take? I can't take any more," I screamed.

A pitiful voice came from the back of the car, and Tommy said, "Please don't yell at me anymore."

God convicted me right then and there for being so cruel to my husband. I felt like absolute pond scum.

"I'm sorry, honey," I said. "You just hold tight. I'll have you at the hospital in no time."

I pulled up to the emergency entrance and ran in to get some help. An attendant followed me out with a wheelchair, and he took one look at Tommy's ankle and said, "Hold on. I'd better get more help."

Miracles and Grace in an Unlikely Place

Two attendants got Tommy onto a gurney, wheeled him into emergency, and put him in a room right away. We were informed that they were going to have to call for an X-ray technician and it would take a little while. Tommy groaned and looked absolutely pitiful.

"Can't you give him something for pain?" I asked.

"He looks to me like he's had quite a bit of painkiller already," the attendant replied.

"Yes, he has. He was drinking sake bombs, among other things."

It was thirty minutes before they took Tommy to X-ray his ankle. I waited in the emergency room, and when they brought him back they said it looked like he'd broken his ankle in at least two places. They would have to wait until morning to do the surgery, because they had to be sure the alcohol was out of his system before they put him under anesthesia. Since there was nothing I could do at the hospital, and he wasn't going anywhere, I kissed Tommy on his forehead and went home.

"Why, Lord, why?" I started screaming on my way home. I couldn't believe that a bar stool could do that much damage. I was close to tears, and then it occurred to me: This was what needed to happen so that Tommy would quit drinking. As a matter of fact, I was sure of it.

"Sorry, Lord," I said. "It's not up to me to question your ways. I'm sure good will come out of this situation. Please forgive me for doubting you, and for being so mean to my husband."

When I got home I called Jeana and told her about the situation. She said that she would keep Tommy in her prayers. "And you, too," she added.

※ ※ ※

Tommy's surgery was not booked until ten o'clock the next morning, so I went to the bar and took care of the banking before going to see my husband. I arrived at the hospital and was informed that they finally found him sober enough to administer pain medication. Still, he looked absolutely pathetic lying there in the bed. My heart went out to him. The guilt that overwhelmed me for my bad behavior the night before manifested itself in compassion that I wasn't aware I was capable of. This, too, had to be from God.

"Hi, honey. How are you feeling?" I asked.

"Not too good—better since they gave me something for the pain. I had too many sake bombs in me earlier and they couldn't give me anything."

"You bet you did, you big oaf. Do you even remember what happened?"

"I remember you screaming at me on the way to the hospital."

"You would remember that. I'm sorry. I was so peeved, because I told you to go home, and when you showed up at the bar I couldn't believe it."

"I was looking for you."

"You didn't need to look for me. I told you exactly where I was going. I shouldn't have let you drive in the first place. Not that I was in any shape to do it. Talk about a buzz kill."

"I'm sorry. I know I'm a butthead sometimes."

"Yeah, but you're my butthead. This will be a great opportunity for you to dry out. No Jack Daniel's in the hospital."

About that time an attendant came in and said, "Time for surgery."

I kissed my honey and he was wheeled away. As I watched him go through the double doors I prayed that God would take care of him. He spent four hours in surgery.

The doctor said that things went well, but there was quite a mess inside of Tommy's ankle. It was broken in three places, and it required a plate and nine screws to put it back together. Recovery would take months.

I couldn't help but think about all of the plans that would be screwed up, like our Daytona trip in early March, that was probably shot to hell. The doctor said it would be a little while before Tommy came out of the anesthesia, but that I could wait in recovery with him. I had just about finished reading a book by T. D. Jakes called *He-Motions*, and I prayed that Tommy would read it while he was stuck on the couch recovering. To use Jakes's own words, it was "a guidebook to help every man understand his own emotional inner workings, and to offer biblically inspired direction toward being the man that God wants him to be." I thought that the subject matter and the timing could not be better. The fixer was still hard at work.

Tommy woke up after about thirty minutes, looked over at me, and gave me a very weak smile.

"How are you doing, honey?" I asked. "The doctor says the surgery went well, although your ankle was quite a mess. You broke the darn thing in three places, on a bar stool. Go figure."

About that time Tommy's surgeon came in.

"Well, hello, there, Tom," he said. "You did quite a job on that ankle of yours. We got it put back together for you, though. I had to put in a plate and quite a few screws, but after a few months of therapy you should be fine. Some people opt to have the hardware taken out eventually, but every situation is different. We'll probably keep you here for one or two more nights to keep an eye on things."

"Great," I said. "He can get all of that booze out of his system."

"He can have a little something if he needs to. We wouldn't want him getting the DTs," the doctor said.

I was mortified. I wanted to slap that doctor upside his head.

"He's been here for almost two days and he hasn't had a problem. Why would it be an issue now? What better place than a hospital is there to dry out?" I pronounced.

"Let's just take care of that ankle for now," the doctor said. "One step at a time. I'll come by and check on you tomorrow. Now get some rest."

I was fuming. How could a doctor tell my husband that it was okay to have a pop if he needed it? He was supposed to be looking out for my husband's welfare, for pity's sake.

"I don't care what that stupid doctor says," I told Tommy as soon as he'd left the room. "You've come this far, and this would be a great time to quit. You said yourself that you know you need to. Please, honey, Doc Coelho told you that eighty percent of your problems were related to alcohol. You're in here because you tripped over a damn bar stool."

"Okay, okay. We'll see how it goes. Right now I just need some sleep."

Am I Finally Getting a Break?

"I'll wait with you until they get you to your room. I read this book while waiting for you to get through surgery. It's really great. I'll leave it so you have something to read in your room. It's by T. D. Jakes. It's called *He-Motions*."

"Give me a break, Joyce Junior. I just came out of surgery."

"What? I'm just leaving you something to read that I think will help you. You're going to be stuck in a bed for a while, and the hospital television has so few stations."

An attendant walked in to take Tommy to his room, and that was the end of the conversation. Once Tommy was situated in his room, I left the book on the table next to the bed, kissed him, and went to work.

* * *

God instructed me to be compassionate toward my husband, and for the first couple of weeks it wasn't very hard. I'd removed all the liquor from the house while Tommy was still in the hospital, and I planned on making him as comfortable as possible while he dried out and got well. Every day before I left for work I made sure he had everything he needed: water, pain pills, juice, and plenty of food. I made sandwiches and had chips, yogurt, cottage cheese, and fruit all easily accessible.

I came home early every day and fixed him a nice dinner, and brought home movies, and spent evenings with him on the couch. Tommy acted surprised, even like he felt guilty because I was taking such good care of him.

When I took him to his first doctor's appointment, the doctor said that he should try to start getting around with the crutches more and get a little exercise. He also prescribed some lithium to be sure that Tommy didn't get DTs. I could hardly understand why that was necessary, since Tommy hadn't had a drink in two weeks and seemed to be okay.

Naive little Charisse—I had always been good at turning a blind eye to what I didn't want to see. I had no idea that well-meaning friends had brought Tommy airline bottles of Jack Daniel's to the hospital, or that my invalid husband who couldn't get off the couch managed to get himself into his truck and down to Rite Aid for small bottles of vodka and Jack Daniel's. To this day I don't know where he stashed them. I just know that I was a fool.

* * *

One day Tommy asked me to get him some ice cream.

"I'm sorry, honey; I forgot to buy some. I don't think we have any," I said.

"I'm pretty sure there's some in there," Tommy told me.

"Well, what do you know," I said as I opened the freezer. "I didn't know this was in here."

When a new flavor miraculously showed up in the freezer again a few days later, I confronted Tommy.

"I know this wasn't in here before," I told him. "Where did it come from?"

"I really wanted some ice cream the other day, so I went down to Rite Aid."

"You got in your truck, drove to Rite Aid, and hobbled around the store for ice cream?"

"Yep."

"What kind of an idiot do you think I am? Do you really expect me to believe that you went to all that trouble for ice cream? I've been waiting on you hand and foot, and you've been well enough to take your happy ass to Rite Aid?"

"Remember, the doctor said a little exercise was good for me."

"Don't give me that crap. You've been taking advantage of me, but that's going to stop. I've been jumping through hoops to see to it that you're okay, and you've been playing me. Now that I know you can get around, you can take care of yourself. I'm finished."

After bringing Tommy his pillow so that he could stay on the couch, I went to bed fuming. I hated feeling like a fool. I was mad at Tommy and God.

"Okay, God," I prayed, "I did what you said. I showed my husband compassion; I took care of him and was a supportive wife. This is the thanks I get? What more do you want me to do? How much

Am I Finally Getting a Break?

more to you want me to take? Haven't I entrusted Tommy to your care? Haven't I believed that you will get him to stop drinking?"

As I lay there with angry tears rolling down my face, I heard Joyce in my head saying, "Let go and let God. Your joy comes from God and does not depend on any person. If you are not at peace, you are not depending on God."

I certainly was not at peace. I prayed a fervent prayer.

"God, I want the peace that surpasses understanding. Please take these burdens from me. I can't do this anymore. Tommy is yours, God. I'm his wife, and I'll stay beside him if he drinks himself to death. I love him, and I love You. I need Your help. I can't do this on my own."

A quiet stillness settled over me, and I felt God was saying, *That's all I needed to hear, my child.*

I threw off the blankets, jumped up, went to the living room, and told Tommy to come to bed. He looked a little dismayed, but he hobbled down the hall behind me. Once in bed, by the grace of God I wrapped my arms around him and went to sleep. Nothing brings serenity like following the Lord's promptings.

* * *

My newfound peace was exhilarating. Jeannie couldn't believe the difference in me on our walks. No more crying, whining, and poor-me talk. I told her about my experience with God the night before, but she wasn't in the same place as me spiritually, so she didn't really understand. She didn't need to understand it; she just knew that I was happier and more at peace, and she was thankful for that.

I went with Tommy to his next doctor's appointment, and he said that Tommy's ankle was looking good. I thought it was still way too swollen, but the doctor said that was normal.

"We're supposed to be leaving for Daytona, Florida, next month. Do you think it'll be okay for him to go?" I asked. "Our plane tickets are already bought and paid for."

"I don't think he'll be up to walking on the beach, but he should be all right as long as he doesn't spend too much time on his feet."

DAYTONA BIKE WEEK, 2004

Traveling with someone in a wheelchair actually made things a lot easier. We got to get on the plane first, and I was able to load bags onto Tommy's lap and zip around the airport. When we changed planes in Dallas there was another chair waiting for us, and I wheeled Tommy to lunch and then to our gate. I was having fun pushing him around. When we got to Orlando I wheeled him outside, where our friends John and Linda waited to take us to their house. We hadn't seen them since they left Hollister; they were a big part of the Johnny's family, and we looked forward to spending time with them. We planned on staying a couple of days at the rally and a couple of days with our friends. It was raining when we left Hollister, and Florida was gorgeous.

    Daytona Bike Week was a lot different from the Hollister rally. For starters, it was much more spread out. Bikes filled the main drag, and all the bars had tubs of beer on ice set up along the sidewalks in front of them. There was a real laid-back atmosphere. I assumed that people would know all about Hollister and Johnny's, but very few did. There was no rock-star status for the owners of Johnny's in Daytona. We searched out the large vendor area where

Corbin Motorcycle Seats and Biker Design were set up, stopping at different bars so Tommy could rest his leg. Tom from Biker Design was too busy to visit, but he told his people to take good care of us. He made and sold our Johnny's T-shirts during our rally, and got the room for us in Daytona. I recognized a few of his employees who'd worked our rally, and they gave me a great deal on a pile of shirts for my entire crew.

After shopping, we took our things back to the car and found a place to eat dinner close to where it was parked. Tommy was in agony, so after dinner he opted to go back to the hotel room with the car. My friends and I stayed out to see what the nightlife was like during the rally, and what I witnessed was nothing I would want to see in Hollister. Women in nothing but G-strings and high heels danced on high-top tables, and most of the bartenders had very little more on. There was a real Sodom and Gomorrah feeling that wasn't comfortable for me. It gave me a better appreciation for our rally, which was fun without getting smutty. I liked the idea that ours was different, and I hoped that it would stay that way.

RECOVERY- WE'RE JUST GETTING STARTED

MOWING DOWN MAILBOXES

Back on the home front, Tommy and I enjoyed each other more, and things were good. Once Tommy's ankle got better and he could get around more easily, he started hitting the bottle pretty hard again. It wasn't long before he was back in the saddle and pretty much drunk all the time. As I'd heard in Al-Anon, every time an alcoholic goes back to drinking, his condition accelerates and he's worse off than he was before. Cutting back after his hospital stay only led to his hitting it even harder when he felt better.

I wanted to moan and complain and beg him to stop, but I had already been around that mountain and was not about to do it again. When I came home and Tommy was a miserable grouch, I went to our room and read. He could grumble and complain all he wanted, but he wasn't stealing my joy. Things were going pretty well at the bar, and since I was no longer whining all the time, people enjoyed hanging with me. I can honestly say that the day I came home and found ours and the neighbors' mailboxes mowed down, Tommy didn't even cross my mind.

I walked in the door at about six thirty and I said, "Hey, someone ran over the mailboxes."

Mowing Down Mailboxes

"I don't want to hear about it," Tommy growled at me. "I've been online looking for a rehab to get into."

"You drove over the mailboxes?"

"Yeah, I ran over the mailboxes. I know I need help. I'll find a program. I'll get into a program."

He stormed down the hall, and I wasn't sure what I should do. I waited for ten minutes and he never came back to the front of the house, so I went online and looked for a rehabilitation center. I was thankful to find the Camp Recovery Center in the Santa Cruz Redwoods. I called and they said they could admit Tommy in four days if he was interested. I didn't want him to lose his resolve and knew we needed to move fast. I told them I would talk to my husband and call them in the morning. I thanked Jesus that there was light at the end of the tunnel for my husband. I crawled into bed, wrapped my arms around Tommy, and, despite the smell of stale Jack Daniel's, I went blissfully to sleep.

Tommy got up early the next morning and I heard the sound of ice cubes hitting the glass. I hated the sound and hoped that soon it would be the last time. I joined Tommy in the kitchen and he was brewing coffee.

"I spent some time online last night," I told him. "I think I found a great place for you, if you want to go. It's in the Santa Cruz Mountains. It's a thirty-day program, and they said they could take you in on Thursday. I just need to give them all of our medical insurance information."

"Our insurance will cover it?"

"All but thirty-two hundred dollars; they said they would take that in two payments: one when they sign you up and the other halfway into your treatment."

"That's a lot of money. What if you spend all that money and then it doesn't work? I hear all the time about people in and out of treatment."

"That's a chance I'm willing to take. I believe that God helped me to find this place. They said it was highly unusual that they had an opening, but someone left early. I think it's a sign. I've got the money in savings, and I can't think of a better way of spending it. You just give me the word."

"I've got to fix the mailboxes and square away a few things. I guess Thursday will work, though."

"I'll see if Syl can work so I can take you there."

"Don't do that. I've been talking off and on to a guy named Tom whom I got ahold of one night when I called the AA emergency help line. I'm sure he'd be glad to get me there."

"You called the AA emergency help line? I had no idea."

"There's a lot you don't know. Don't worry about getting me to rehab. I'd really rather get there by myself, honey. Just leave me the information and I'll take care of the rest."

THE CAMP RECOVERY CENTER

I left his admission in Tommy's hands, and he arranged to check into rehab on Thursday, November 5. When I kissed him good-bye to go to work Thursday morning I knew I wouldn't get to see him for at least ten days. Visitations were allowed only on Sundays, and they wanted him settled in before I went to see him. I could talk to him only once a day on a pay phone, because cell phones were not allowed. I was scared for him, but I knew he was in God's hands. I had been saying for a long time that Tommy would quit drinking. I believed it was God's plan for him. Now that it might really be happening, it was surreal.

I knew I would miss Tommy, but I was thrilled that he was getting help. And I had nothing to do with it. I was actually a little surprised at myself. I'd done such a good job of leaving Tommy in God's hands that I never thought about it being him who mowed down the mailboxes. Back in the day he would have been the first person I thought of.

"I have come a long way; thank you, Jesus," I said out loud.

* * *

Miracles and Grace in an Unlikely Place

With Tommy gone for thirty days I planned on staying busy at the bar and doing a lot of reading and writing. I hoped I'd make some headway on my book. I hadn't worked on it for so long that I didn't remember where I left off. Stopping and starting over and over again was really slowing down the process. Whoever said writing was easy never attempted to write a book.

When the Sunday visitation rolled around, I was so wound up that I couldn't see straight. I'd packed up the laundry list of things my husband told me he needed in our early morning conversation. We usually talked at about six thirty, when there wasn't a line of people waiting to use the pay phone.

I found a picnic basket that had been tucked away in the closet for years. It had a nice little red-and-white-checked tablecloth in it and a set of red plastic silverware and dishes to match. I packed up a wonderful meal for the two of us, and I felt like Little Red Riding Hood when I approached the check-in area with my basket. I told the attendant that I was there to see Thomas Horsfall.

"They just finished group," the nice counselor informed me. "I'll get someone to tell him you're here."

I checked out the scenery while I waited for Tommy, and it looked like a tranquil place for rehab. There were redwoods everywhere, and lots of grassy areas with huge wooden carvings of forest animals. A long driveway led to the two- and three-story lodges that housed the patients. Watching Tommy coming toward me down that long driveway was like something out of a movie. I didn't know whether to wait for him or run to him. I decided on the former so that I didn't embarrass him. As he approached I couldn't help but notice how exhausted and frail he looked. I threw my arms around him and kissed him repeatedly.

"I've missed you so much," I told him.

"I've missed you, too. Did you bring my stuff?"

"It's all in the car: pillow, sweats, shoes, and Bible. I couldn't carry all of it and our lunch."

"That's a big basket. What the heck have you got in there?"

"A little bit of everything. I didn't know what you felt like eating, and I wanted to cover my bases."

"I don't want to disappoint you, but I haven't been real hungry. They took me to the emergency room again yesterday because my blood pressure dropped so low."

"My poor honey. Are you okay?"

"They tell me I'll live. I guess I was a pretty hard case to detox. They've got me on meds four times a day. They promise it will get better."

We ate our lunch in the sun. Tommy ate very little. Then we took his stuff to get checked in. The Camp scrutinized everything that came through the gate, and Tommy informed me that two people had already been tossed for not following the rules.

"Some people have been back here two and three times," he said. "I only plan on doing this once."

"I'm thrilled to hear that, honey."

As I drove away from the Camp I was both happy and sad. I felt bad leaving my husband looking so haggard and worn-out, and missed him by the time I hit the highway. I was also elated that he was finally getting help.

* * *

The following week I made Tommy some of my spaghetti and garlic bread. I wrapped it up and put it in an ice chest to stay warm. I picked Allen up and was grateful that for once he was ready on time. We talked on the way there about what a transition it was going to be for all of us with Tommy not drinking.

Since my boozing husband was all my son had ever known, he couldn't even wrap his mind around it, and he cried when he saw Tommy. Allen gave him a big bear hug, and Tommy told him not to be upset because it was all good. We enjoyed our meal together, and Tommy gave us a short tour, after which he walked us to the car and picked up the week's necessities. As we drove off, Allen was very emotional.

"It's okay, son. Tommy is doing fine. He looks a lot better than last week. If you'd seen him then you would really be freaking out."

"I know. I just hate seeing him like that. We might fight, but you know we really love each other."

"Yes, I do, and you should be happy. If Tommy didn't quit he was going to die just like Danny. I hope you've learned something from all of this and you don't go down the same path. I'm so sorry we exposed you to the lifestyle."

"Don't worry, Mom; I don't plan on being an alcoholic."

"Nobody plans on it, son."

* * *

There was no doubt in my mind that Tommy would see recovery. I would have only one more visit with him at the Camp, and that was on family day. Family members were invited to sit in on group and hear how their loved ones felt about their recovery, and everyone was invited to share. It was one heck of an eye-opener for me. People had nasty drug addictions that caused them to do terrible things. Listening to the horror stories from family members who suffered through numerous incarcerations, violence, and thievery from the people they loved made me feel like a wimp. Tommy's issue was nothing compared to some of those people's.

When it came time for Tommy to share I felt very blessed by what he had to say about me. He told everyone how thankful he was that I put up with his drinking for so many years and kept faith in him. I sat and cried through his share. Then I talked about some of my codependency issues and told everyone that we never would have made it without God. The peoplewho embraced God seemed to have a lot more hope. I left that day wondering how any of those people would make it without His help. I was thankful Tommy knew who his higher power was.

* * *

On Saturday, December 3, 2005, I went to the Camp to bring Tommy home. Mom and I had gone through the entire house and Tommy's shop while he was in rehab and thrown away every bottle of booze we could find. There must have been hundreds of empty Jack Daniel's bottles in every size, from a liter to 187 milliliters. There were many vodka bottles, too, but Jack was the big find of the day. We filled two thirty-two-gallon garbage cans with them. Anytime we found a bottle with a drop in it we poured it out. It was a rude awakening for me to see just how bad Tommy's disease had become, and a huge testament to the miracle-working power of prayer.

    I stocked the fridge with groceries and the freezer with ice cream so that we could enjoy our first weekend together at home without even leaving the house. Tommy informed me that he would be leaving to go to meetings. A meeting a day for ninety days, he told me. I don't think he missed one for six months.

SOBRIETY AND AN AWARD- IT DOESN'T GET MUCH BETTER THAN THAT

What a way to start 2006. Tommy was sober and Johnny's Bar & Grill won the chamber of commerce's Hospitality Business of the Year award. Johnny's was the first bar to win the honor, and I was over the moon. A lot of people still thought of Johnny's as a biker bar and never bothered to have a meal in our place. I was looking forward to using the opportunity to grab some new customers. The awards event for three hundred or so people was going to be held at the San Juan Oaks Golf Club on January 22, 2006. I had to look good, and my speech needed to be exceptional. I had so much to be thankful for. God gave me a top-notch crew that helped me to make Johnny's into the popular place that it was. My husband was sober, and I was so proud of him.

Sobriety and an Award- It Doesn't Get Much Better Than That

The 2006 award winning Johnny's team

Tommy had been out of rehab for only a little more than a month, and I wondered whether a night out with everyone drinking around him would be too much for him. I told him that I would understand if he didn't want to go, but he insisted that he would be fine. Bonus—now I had a designated driver. Tommy, the DD for the evening? It was almost too much to take in. He even agreed to pick up our cook, Rey, and his wife, Lori, so they wouldn't have to worry about driving home after drinking.

I tore through my closet trying to find the right thing to wear. This was a big occasion, and I wanted to look fabulous.

Tommy had a tux that he bought when he'd joined the Elks Lodge years earlier, and he still looked great in it. But I didn't have a clue what to wear. I very seldom bought clothes for myself, and I couldn't see spending a bunch of money on a dress that I would wear one time. I had only a few dresses that still fit my more full figured midlife body. After much searching I chose a long red dress that I'd ordered out of a catalog but had never worn. It had hints of silver throughout, and was stylish and sexy—maybe a little too sexy. The slit on the side that went to the bottom of my hip wasn't so bad, but the spaghetti straps and plunging neckline took it a little too far into the wow zone. I found a silver jacket that matched perfectly that would cover the lack of material in the back, but it didn't do much to disguise the swooping neckline. It was beautiful, though, and I really had nothing else to wear. I took it off and tried to find something else, but over and over again I came back to that red dress.

There was a time when I wouldn't have given a second thought to wearing something low-cut. "God, why do you have to affect every decision I make now?" I whined. I reasoned with Him and myself that it was just one night out. Then I thought about the speech I had written. I thanked God and gave Him all the credit for my success because of the employees He provided me with and the blessings He bestowed upon me. I said I would be nothing if it weren't for God always looking out for me. I was already going to throw people off guard because so many find it hard to believe that a bar owner can be a Christian. Would the dress detract from what I was saying? The third time I put it on, I left it on.

"I'm sorry, Lord," I said, "but I have no choice. Please help me to do well tonight and give a good speech that honors You."

I practiced my speech while putting on my makeup and curling my hair. I'd worked on it for weeks and was determined not to skip half of what I wanted to say. I truly believed that God hand-picked all of my employees for me. Their individual qualities made Johnny's a well-oiled machine. I had no idea how they'd stayed with me through the early years, when I was a controlling and overbearing tyrant. I was a more grateful person now, and this was my big chance to let them know publicly how much they meant to me.

I took a last look in the mirror and was pleased with what I saw. I was fashionably sexy. Tommy was waiting for me in the living room, and I was hoping he'd tell me I looked great.

Instead he said, "Whoa, that dress is a little low, don't you think?"

Sobriety and an Award- It Doesn't Get Much Better Than That

"That's it. I'm changing. I don't have any nice clothes. You're in a tux, and this is the only formal dress that I have that fits, and I thought I looked nice."

"I'm sorry, honey. Don't change; you do look nice. In fact, you look great."

"Why couldn't you have said that in the first place instead of making me self-conscious?"

"Because I'm just a dumb guy," he said as he wrapped his arms around me. "You're going to be the best-looking woman there. Now let's get out of here before we're late."

"Now you're overdoing it. It's just that I want everything to be perfect tonight. This is such an honor, and I don't want anything to take away from it."

* * *

When the Johnny's crew was in attendance, I made a toast to our group and thanked everyone for coming. We laughed and told stories through dinner, which helped take the edge off. I was so nervous that I didn't even feel the four glasses of wine I had to drink. As soon as the evening's official tapped her glass with a spoon, my heart started pounding and my palms started sweating. There were so many people there. This group was a far cry larger than the city council meetings I spoke at.

When our bar and my name were announced I looked at Tommy and he looked exasperated. He wasn't mentioned at all. Even though he didn't help in the day-to-day running of the bar, his not being mentioned at all was like a punch in the gut. I had always been the workhorse and the face of Johnny's, so deep down I didn't understand his irritation. I could see a cauldron of old resentments brewing, and I was scared to death that he would have a drink as he got more annoyed about the situation.

I got to the podium with my speech in hand and said a silent prayer. I followed my notes as far as I know, but the speech was a big blur to me. I finished speaking, heard the applause, and went back to my seat. All of my employees thanked me and said what a great job I did. I was thrilled that the hard part was over and now

Miracles and Grace in an Unlikely Place

I was in party mode. Tommy, however, was miserable. After the award ceremony we all headed to the bar for dancing. Tommy decided to go home and come back for me later. I had a wonderful time with my crew, and when the music stopped it was midnight, way past Tommy's bedtime, so I was very grateful when he picked me up.

ALCOHOLICS ANONYMOUS AND GOD

At first I was very happy about Tommy's dedication to AA, but eventually I felt like his recovery was all about AA and not much about God. I tried hard to leave him to God and diligently pray for him. I continued my routine of reading my Bible, going to church, and listening to Joyce. Once in a while Tommy would go to church with me, but he hated the music, so he showed up late. He enjoyed Pastor Henry, and I was glad of that. I wanted badly for him to have a closer and more personal walk with Jesus. At church on Sundays, if you had a need you could pray with one of our intercessors during the worship portion of the service.

I'd been praying with one about Tommy for months. She was a recovering addict and alcoholic and she always gave me hope. I wasn't bashful about praying with her even when Tommy came to church. He tells me now how much he hated knowing I was up there praying for him. Through my four-year spiritual journey, God used Tommy and his disease to work on my flaws. He taught me patience, an issue I continue to struggle with, and He taught me to love people even when you don't like them, which did not always come easily, especially when Thursday nights took a turn for the worse.

GUARDIAN ANGELS EVERYWHERE

HELP ME, LORD; IT'S THURSDAY

Thursdays had always been crazy, but they were a nice, fun kind of crazy. I'm not sure when things changed, because it happened so gradually. Since I had two doormen and two bartenders, I started going home early on Thursdays. I'd leave at about eleven o'clock, after I had the girls all stocked up. Soon it seemed like every Friday morning there was another story about ill-behaving clientele. I finally decided that I'd better hang around and get a handle on things. The first night I stayed on I was appalled at what I saw. At about eleven thirty it was like the entire crowd shifted; the nice regulars were gone and replaced with a bunch of hooligans. When the problems started, a woman was usually at the center of it.

As a Christian I had things that I was not about to tolerate, and women humping one another on the dance floor was one of them. I know it happens all the time in other places, but Johnny's represented me, and I could not condone it. I found myself out on the dance floor pulling women off one another all the time. They would tell me to lighten up, and I would tell them to take a look at the faces of the men who were watching them. "When one of you broads is raped in the parking lot, you'll be asking how such

Help Me, Lord; It's Thursday

a thing could happen to you," I told them. "You are asking for trouble with your crude and disgusting behavior, and you're not going to do it in my house," I screeched.

I screamed a lot in those days. I had to put a sign on the ladies' room door that said, ONE LADY AT A TIME OR RISK THE WRATH OF THE REDHEAD. They were going in groups of two and three and doing God only knows what. I hung a sign on the deejay booth that stated, FOUL LANGUAGE IS NOT PERMITTED WHEN SINGING A SONG. People had begun screaming the F-word into the microphone.

The drug activity had been one of my big blind spots; I didn't want to believe that anyone would do such a thing in my place. I now had to face the fact that the problem was really out of control. I regularly kicked in the men's room door and yelled, "All of you bastards get out of my bar." My language had pretty much gone to hell in a handbag on Thursday nights. The gang element moved in, and guys in wife-beaters and white T-shirts with their hats on backward were regularly a problem. It was difficult not to stereotype people when the bad behavior I witnessed always came from people with the same look.

In the good old days Ray Wood did walk-throughs and visited without my having to ask. Now when I called the dispatcher for a walk-through, I specifically asked that the officers be casual so the bangers wouldn't know I called. But the darn cops always walked right in and asked to speak with the owner.

When it came to anyone disrespecting me or my bar I was a crazy and fearless wench. Once I saw red I was gone. I didn't care how big or scary the individual was, if you acted up in my house you were confronted by the redhead. There is no doubt in my mind that God has a couple of guardian angels working overtime to keep an eye on me. I guess I was getting a little too big for my britches, so they decided to step aside one night.

I happened upon a man who was obviously posturing for a fight, and I stepped right in between him and his opponent, stood on my tippytoes, and said, "Not in my place you don't. . . ." The next thing I knew I woke up on the floor with Linda, who was now doing my karaoke, standing over me. "Charisse, are you all right?" I remember looking for my shoe and wondering how I wound up on the floor. This guy must have been on PCP, because he tossed me like a rag doll. A disabled customer witnessed the entire episode from his wheelchair next to the karaoke booth. If I'd been thrown at a different angle I would have landed in his lap.

The bar was in complete chaos. People were running all over the place, and the man who tossed me was now outside. I called the cops from my cell phone while I was still on the floor. A lot of people left the bar, including the disabled guy, who went to his truck. He must have had a lift to get into it, because it was a really tall four-by-four. How it happened I'll never understand, but somehow the man who tossed me ended up on the disabled man's hood in the parking lot behind the bar.

My disabled knight in shining armor drove down our alley going the wrong direction and slammed on the brakes, tossing the hoodlum into San Benito Street. He then proceeded to drive over him, not once but twice. People were running and screaming everywhere. When I made it outside to talk to the police after the little birdies stopped circling my head, an officer asked whether I recognized the man who had accosted me. I said, "Yes, I think I do. It's the man sitting in the middle of the street handcuffed with blood running down his face."

* * *

Another night we had an incident with a man who was known to be a white supremacist. He made a racial comment to a Hispanic man on our patio and he got jumped by at least six guys. They were beating him bloody, and I was trying to pull guys off of him and screaming at the top of my lungs, "Call the cops. Call the cops." By the time my second bouncer made it to the patio to help, all hell was breaking loose. Jeana had the sense to grab the hose, and we had to spray everyone down to keep from having a full-blown riot. I was sick to death of the problems, and begged the Hollister Police Department to do a walk-through every Thursday night at eleven. I didn't care how much money we were ringing up; I didn't want that element in my bar and I didn't know how to get rid of them.

* * *

Help Me, Lord; It's Thursday

One Thursday I went to see Wynonna Judd in concert with a good friend and customer. On returning home we got stuck on Highway 25 because of construction. While we were sitting in the car on the highway a brawl broke out at the bar, and it wasn't even eleven p.m. Some Hollister gangbangers and some Watsonville boys had an altercation and it got ugly. Jeana called me on my cell phone and said that she'd called the police and closed the bar immediately.

When I reviewed the video of the incident the following day I was horrified. One gangster had a man on the ground and was repeatedly slugging him in the face while onlookers stood by. If I had been there I would have been on his back scratching his eyes out, I was sure. Poor Linda had her table knocked completely over by some thugs trying to exit the building, and her CDs scattered everywhere. She was a basket case over the ordeal, and skipped doing karaoke for two Thursdays to recover. The gang element was easy to identify, and I had all of the creeps' faces on tape. I burned them onto a DVD and turned it over to the Hollister PD. I never heard a thing about them picking up the gangsters. As far as I know they didn't even view the video.

We never had problems like that on Friday nights. We had a nice, laid-back, older crowd whom Linda enjoyed playing for, but she began to hate Thursdays.

I was fit to be tied, and getting no help from the local authorities. I had to do something to discourage that element from coming into the bar. I established a new dress code that irritated some of the regulars. Every Thursday night I paced, watching everyone like a hawk, and anyone who even looked like trouble was asked to leave. God's protection continued, and it amazed me how many times he put me in the right place at the right time.

* * *

One night I was standing at the bar when a wench grabbed a beer bottle and was poised to hit another woman over the head with it. I don't even remember lifting my arm up, but I had the bottle in my hand and that bi-yatch out the door before she knew what happened.

I could go on and on, but I'm thrilled to say that eventually we got a handle on things. If it weren't for God's protection I can't imagine what would have happened to me at Johnny's. In all my years as owner, the problems have been rare, and most of the crazy stuff took place after 2008. I'm so thankful that we are still known as a friendly little place that ladies feel comfortable coming to by themselves. Thursdays got a lot quieter; we have a lot less business than we used to, but not having the problems that go along with big business is worth it to me.

HIS TIMING, NOT MINE

I had the crazy idea that once Tommy got sober, everything would be hunky-dory. Boy, was I wrong. His cranky demeanor didn't disappear. In fact, at times I think it was worse. At first it was as if he were mad at the world because he couldn't drink anymore and other people still could, which brings us to my drinking habits. I was truly ready, willing, and able to quit drinking if I needed to for Tommy. I don't think God would have moved in him if I hadn't made the decision to do whatever it took to help my husband. Not only did Tommy not ask me to quit drinking; he didn't want me to. He knew I had a bar to run, and he didn't expect me to do it without drinking. It was truly a gift of grace, because not only is it difficult to hang out with a bunch of people who are drinking and not join them, but some customers are actually offended when I won't have a drink with them.

Back to the cranky, angry-at-the-world stuff: The tiniest little things set Tommy off when he was a drunk, and they continued to do so when he got sober. If something fell off of the sink and landed on the floor he yelled, "F***." If he tripped over the cat he yelled, "F***." If the batteries were dead in the remote he yelled,

"F***." I had long since stopped using the F-word; I despised it, asked customers and employees not to use it, and it was like nails on a chalkboard to me every time he said it. I'd ask him not to use it and he'd say, "Leave me alone, Joyce Junior." Still battling the whole mouth issue, I went on a tangent about how ugly the word was and how ugly he looked when he said it.

I was thrilled that my man was sober, but now I had a sober grouch for a husband. When something around the house needed fixing it was still like pulling teeth to get him to do it. At first I didn't ask him to fix things around the bar, but when he started eating there I figured he could do repairs, but as usual he hated doing any work at Johnny's.

* * *

I was in the midst of trying to handle my problems gracefully when Jeannie moved to Oakdale. Since I couldn't bend her ear personally, I did it via my cell phone while on my walk. I went on and on about how Tommy was such a miserable bugger, and she was always very supportive. Then one day I got into my car and turned on Joyce, and her sermon was about complaining about the things we want to see change instead of praying about them. It was by no means the first time I'd heard her preach on the subject, but this time it hit home.

She said, "You want things to change but all you do is talk about it, think about it, think about it, talk about it, and think about it some more. You will never see change if you don't ask God for what you want and expect to see it come to pass. So the next time you want to complain about your problems, go to the throne, not the phone."

God once again used Joyce to knock some sense into my head. Whenever I listen to her and heed her advice I am grateful. I made a decision right then and there that I was not going to complain about my husband, not even to my best friend. Romans 4 of the Bible, tells us to call those things that are not as though they are. I hung the scripture up on my mirror at home. I hung it at my desk at work. I even put it in my glove box and I repeated it daily. Just like the lost Israelites who took forty years to make an eleven-day trip, I kept going around the same mountain where my husband was concerned. I wanted to get it right so I wouldn't have to continue dealing with the same old issues. My trials with my husband kept me closely connected to God, because I came to realize that without His help I couldn't get through a single day—not even an hour. He showed up in ways I never expected.

AN INTERVENTION

The karaoke crowd was filling up the bar, and I spotted a young man I hadn't seen in a long time. I was sure he was the man who left me with a $40 tab years earlier. The money was not the issue. I let him run a tab in good faith that he would pay me back, and I never forget someone who takes advantage of my trust, especially someone I had treated like a son. I approached his table unsure of his name, but convinced that he was the long-lost customer who owed me money. He recognized me right away and stood up to give me a hug.

"Hi, there, how are you doing? You look great," he said.

"You, too—it's been years. How are you doing?"

"I'm great. I don't live in town anymore but it hasn't been years since I've been here."

"I may have missed you when you came in before. Did you know you left me with a forty-dollar tab?"

"Really, I thought I paid my tab the last time I was here, but if I owe you I'll make good on it."

"Thank you; I appreciate that." He acted like he genuinely did not remember the tab, so I felt better about him right away.

An Intervention

"When's the last time you saw Rick?" I asked, remembering that they worked together and were inseparable the last time he hung out at Johnny's.

"Rick who?" was his response.

"Rick who? You guys worked together, and he was like a big brother to you."

"Are you sure you don't have me mixed up with someone else? I'm Victor."

"Oh, my gosh, I'm so embarrassed. You aren't who I thought you were, so you don't owe me any money. Please let me buy you a drink to apologize."

I felt like an idiot, but I had no idea that a case of mistaken identity would lead to one of the wildest experiences I would have at Johnny's. We went up to the bar and one of Jeana's signature drinks, the purple hooter, became two, and the dice cups came out, which led to two more. We bonded over cocktails, and even though I didn't remember Victor well, it felt like we had known each other for a very long time.

He confessed that he had been away because he was in jail for drug charges. He told me that he'd screwed up his entire life. He was beaten down and defeated. As God often does, He led me to talk to Victor about Jesus. There I was, a few drinks under my belt, talking to a guy about my Lord and Savior. I told him that we all make mistakes, but that God is in the business of forgiveness, and that when we are truly sorry for what we do and repent, He always forgives us and gives us a clean slate. I told him that God had completely transformed my life, and assured him that his life could be renewed, too. Victor said that he had been too bad and done too much, and I told him that even murderers can be forgiven. I must have struck a chord, because he wound up confessing to me that he was at Johnny's to kill a man.

"What the heck do you mean, you're supposed to kill somebody?" I asked.

"I owe some really bad people money for drugs, and I don't have the money to pay them back. If I kill the other guy who owes them, my debt will be erased. Otherwise they are going to kill me."

"You can't be serious. You're not a murderer. I know you're not. You just can't do it."

"I've got the gun they gave me in my pocket. Its serial numbers have been filed off and it's untraceable."

"Victor, you can't do this. You are not a killer. Even if you didn't get caught, you would hate yourself for the rest of your life."

While Victor and I were talking, it was as if we were in a big bubble and everyone else was on the outside of it. I felt like God led me to talk to Victor just for this purpose. I believed that the mistaken identity was no accident; it was ordained. I had to make sure that he didn't do this horrible thing that he would regret the rest of his life. He left briefly to go the bathroom. When he came back, he told me he'd thrown the gun into the Dumpster.

"I can't go back to where I was staying, because they'll be looking for me there. I could check myself into rehab tomorrow. There's a facility in Salinas, and I'd be safe there for a while until I figure out what I'm going to do. I could really use the rehab."

"Where will you stay tonight?"

"I don't know. I need to stay out of sight, and I don't know how I'll get to Salinas tomorrow. Man, have I messed up my life."

"I tell you what: You can come home with me and stay on our couch, and my husband can take you to the rehabilitation center tomorrow. How does that sound?"

The intensity of the situation sobered me up. I felt sharp as a tack and on a mission. I believed that since God led me to this man, He would get us home safely. It was almost last call, and I'd stocked up the bar, so I decided to get out a little early to be safe. I told Jeana that Victor needed my help and that I was going to take him to my house and put him up on our couch. She didn't think it was a very good idea, but she recognizes when I've made my mind up about something. She wished me luck and told me to be safe.

As we walked to my car I found myself looking over my shoulder to be sure that "they" were not watching. I cautiously drove home and we never saw another car on the road between Johnny's and my house, which was highly unusual. When we got home I gave Victor a blanket and a pillow and got him situated on the couch.

I gave him a hug and he said, "I don't know how to thank you."

"Don't thank me; thank God. This is all His doing," I said.

An Intervention

I knew I wouldn't have done what I did on my own in a million years. I believed wholeheartedly that God had arranged the encounter, and I was thrilled to be used by Him. I didn't want to wake Tommy to tell him about Victor, because not only was it a long story, but I knew he'd think I was crazy. I crawled in bed quietly and didn't wake him. I don't know how long I'd been asleep when I heard Tommy yell, "What the f***!"

Victor woke up and, in his drunken haze, didn't remember where he was and needed to use the bathroom. Even though I left a night-light on in the spare bathroom, he wandered into our bedroom. Tommy was looking for his gun and I shot up in bed and yelled, "It's all right, honey; it's just Victor."

"Who the hell is Victor, and what is he doing in our house?"

"He's a friend, honey, and he needed a place to sleep, so I let him stay on our couch. I'll explain the whole thing tomorrow."

I got up and led Victor down the hall. He was clearly confused and didn't know where he was. I reminded him that he was staying at my house and going to rehab in the morning. He still looked a little unsure, so I walked him to the bathroom and then pointed to the couch and reminded him that it was where he was sleeping. I got back into bed and told Tommy that I was sorry that I hadn't told him about Victor, but that I didn't want to wake him.

"I could have shot the guy if my gun had been close enough. Don't ever do that again; do you hear me?"

"I'm sorry, honey. I promise it will never happen again."

"What kind of a crazy story is behind all of this, anyway?"

"It's too crazy to tell you tonight. Let's go back to sleep and I'll explain the whole thing in the morning."

* * *

At seven a.m. my cat jumped on top of me as usual, and even though I had been in bed for only five hours, I could not go back to sleep. Tommy wrapped himself around me like he always did in the morning, and I lay there with my mind spinning. How was he going to take it when I shared my story? He had seen a lot of changes in me and knew how much I loved Jesus and wanted to help people, but he might think this was a little over-the-top. After about ten minutes Tommy asked me, "So why is this strange man sleeping on the couch in our living room?"

"Honey, you're probably going to think I've lost my marbles, but it really is a God thing."

I told him the whole story, and he confirmed that yes, he did think I was crazy. He handled the whole thing really well, and said that he would take Victor to Salinas to the rehabilitation center.

"Thank you, honey; you are doing a very good deed and God will bless you for it."

"He already blessed me with a crazy redhead."

I got up and started breakfast, and Victor woke up to the smell of bacon cooking. Just then Tommy joined us and I made introductions. Victor explained that I stopped him from doing something very stupid, and that I had probably changed his life forever. The guys talked about the recovery center in Salinas, and Victor told Tommy how thankful he was for the ride there.

"I hope it works out for you. My wife has faith in you for some reason, so we'll do what we can to help."

After we ate, Tommy went to warm up his truck, and I gave Victor a huge hug and told him that I would be praying for him. I gave him our address and telephone numbers, and he promised to keep in touch. When Tommy came back in I hugged and kissed him and told him how much I appreciated him.

"I don't know how to thank you guys," Victor said.

"You can thank us by doing well and changing your path, my friend. I'm sure that you can if you ask God for help. You can't do it without Christ."

"You've given me a lot to think about."

As the guys drove off I started to cry. I felt so blessed to be used by God in such an amazing way. A man was alive today, and another one had a new lease on life because God chose to use a tipsy bar owner to intervene for Him.

SURVIVING ANOTHER ROUGH PATCH

AS THE KITCHEN TURNS

It started out as an awesome year but 2006 became a year of tests on a monumental level. I'm pretty amazed that I got through it. Not only was our rally canceled, but I was having serious employee issues. I am very blessed person in that area, but the rough patch in 2006 that I came to refer to as "my six months from hell" almost did me in. Without God's help it would certainly have sent me to the loony bin. This story gives credence to the saying that sometimes truth is stranger than fiction.

I was blessed with Ralph when I bought Johnny's, and he and the two cooks who followed him got us through ten productive years. Outside of a few hiccups and the usual temperamental cook stuff, the restaurant business grew and we were pretty happy. Then Rey Valdez, who was my current cook, got a job at his wife's place of employment. They offered benefits, which I could not afford to provide, and in May of 2006 he gave his notice. Juan, our Saturday cook, said that he was ready to step into Rey's shoes. He was a sweetheart and a good cook, but a little juvenile and irresponsible. Syl and I figured with two mamas working on him we could keep him on the straight and narrow.

As the Kitchen Turns

The first couple of weeks with Juan were great. He was laid-back and sweet and didn't snap at the crew. However, problems surfaced quickly. I told myself he wasn't as conscientious as Rey because he was so young. I had to check up on him daily at the end of his shift to make sure things were done properly. I had to remind him over and over again what needed to be done. Then he started calling in sick and showing up late and looking like he hadn't slept all night.

I confronted him and reminded him that the Fourth of July weekend was fast approaching and that I needed everyone to give their best. He then told me he had committed to a job in Sonora that weekend, which infuriated me. Once again issues were surfacing before a rally. Actually it wasn't even going to be a true rally. The city council put a stop to our motorcycle rally, and preparing for an uncertain Fourth of July weekend was going to be difficult enough. I didn't need cook issues. "What the heck am I supposed to do now?" I wondered out loud. "Dear God, this can't be happening to me, not now."

When Juan went home, I joined Sylvia downstairs and shared my concerns. I had no idea where I would find a cook at such a late date. She told me that Jeana had mentioned that a man came in looking for a cook's job and left a phone number. I was elated and called him as soon as Jeana told me where to find his number. There was no answer, so I left a message on the recorder.

The following morning I was behind the bar when a man came in who looked familiar. Come to find out he'd worked a rally for me years before, but he was an addict back then and left me high and dry on my crucial Saturday morning. I hadn't seen him since, but after we talked for a while I found out that he was clean and sober, and a Christian. Henry apologized profusely for letting me down.

I needed help, so I asked whether he'd like to make up for leaving me in the lurch by helping me out Fourth of July weekend. When he said he'd see if his employer could spare him, I was relieved to see light at the end of the tunnel. Then around two thirty, James, the man who was looking for a cook's job, called. I told him to come on down and talk to me, wondering what other little miracles God had in store. At three thirty a clean-cut-looking guy with a nice smile walked up to the bar and said, "Hi, I'm James." He had a firm handshake and an air of confidence. We had a great conversation, and he told me he would work Fourth of July weekend doing whatever I needed him to do. I silently thanked God, sure that things were finally coming together.

* * *

Henry called on Monday and said that he would be glad to help out during the un-rally. When Juan called in sick again the following Wednesday, I asked Henry whether he was available to fill in. Fortunately he covered Juan. I was sick of Juan's shenanigans, so I offered Henry his job. Syl was not happy about it at all, because she and Henry were like water and oil. I explained to her that I needed someone reliable, and she couldn't argue the fact that Juan was not.

"I just can't explain it, but there's something about Henry that bothers me," Sylvia said.

I didn't listen to her and I hired him anyway. He was a reasonably good cook, but he was as stubborn as a mule. He was determined to do things the way he wanted to do them, not the way we did them, and after she'd worked with him one day, Sylvia's attitude was in the toilet by happy hour. Once again things were not going as I had expected. As Sylvia's stress level rose, so did mine.

THE UN-RALLY OF 2006

Since our city council in their infinite wisdom canceled our rally and I was at a loss as to how many people were coming to town, it made preparations very difficult. If every biker who said that they would be in Hollister for the Fourth of July weekend showed up, we would be as busy as ever. "I wouldn't miss it. This is a tradition," they would tell me. Once attendees shopped at the few vendor tents, the only thing left for them to do was hang out in the restaurants and bars. I was convinced that I would be just as busy as if we had a rally. Especially since the Boozefighters always made Johnny's a destination, rally or no rally. I made multiple trips to San Jose and Costco for supplies. I had one employee after the other call to say that they couldn't work this shift or that shift. The beer cooler broke. The last thing I needed to deal with was another cranky cook situation. I thought that I was going to lose my mind.

The Monday before the Fourth of July weekend, Henry called in sick. Desperate, I called Juan and just about begged him to fill in. I was happy that I fired him in the nicest way possible. The old me would have torn him up before I sent him out the door. I was thankful God had been making changes in my volatile personality. I hung up the phone and almost cried with relief. "Thank you, Jesus," I said.

Juan worked Monday and did a wonderful job. When I walked through the kitchen and heard him and Sylvia joking and laughing it warmed my heart. I hadn't heard that since Henry started working for us. You could cut the tension with a knife when Henry was there. Henry didn't call me by Monday night, so I knew that I needed to make a decision. Did I dare give Juan another chance? Did I have any choice?

I wrapped my arm around Juan's neck and said, "We had a great day today, didn't we?"

"Yeah, we did. I had a good time. I missed Sylvia."

"So what do you say you come back and work for me, but this time you try to act like a responsible adult?"

"Okay, but I still can't work Fourth of July weekend."

"We'll get through it somehow. Just plan on being here for it next year."

* * *

I'd finally gotten planning for the rally down to a science. I had help who came back year after year, and I pretty much knew what to expect as far as business was concerned. Just when I thought I had it dialed, the Hollister City Council pulled the rug out from under me. The only reason the rally didn't show a profit was because of the outrageous law enforcement costs. If the council had the *cojones* to give the chief a budget for law enforcement, the city would make plenty of money during the rally. But the chief was hell-bent on killing our rally. By jacking up the cost of policing the event, he appeared to be succeeding. I was really angry and repeatedly had to ask for forgiveness for wanting to tear the council members limb from limb. In June of 2006 the only thing we talked about at Johnny's was the cancellation of the rally.

"I got more phone calls about the rally today," Sylvia told me.

"I hope you told them to come on down anyway."

The Un-rally of 2006

"Of course I did. And most people say that they will be here. As long as the cops don't screw it up for us, we should have a great weekend even without the rally."

"If" was the operative word. The rumor on the street was that law enforcement had been instructed to give as many tickets as they could for any infraction possible. They had the capacity to ruin our weekend. I couldn't understand why our chief was so opposed to the rally. I talked to him in his office, and he looked me right in the eyes and told me that he wasn't trying to kill our rally, and that instructions to dole out as many tickets as possible were not given. I believe he was lying through his teeth. I hoped that thousands of people would show up anyway. The city was sure to have plenty of law enforcement and no extra sales tax revenue to pay for them. I got hot under the collar every time I thought about it.

* * *

I got to work on Thursday, June 30, at nine a.m. to prepare for the trailer from Budweiser and food deliveries that were arriving early. On my way to Johnny's I saw two event tents and a few vendors set up on private property. The lack of motorcycles and the missing buzz of activity made me sick. I was so angry about our city council turning their backs on our heritage that I wanted to scream. Setting up for the unknown was like starting from scratch in 1996. As I prepared for my weekend of uncertainty, I thanked God for the wonderful crew that He had provided me. Without all of the dedicated members of the Johnny's family I could never get through it. "Well, Lord," I said out loud, "my time is in your hands."

By the time I finished with the banking I heard the roar of motorcycle engines. What a relief. I ran downstairs to see how things were going. The bar was filling up, and there were a few customers at tables. There was no shortage of food, because Pauline, who came back to help despite being seventy-four years old, had done a wonderful job preparing the breakfast buffet.

"Well, boss," she said, "now all we need is customers to eat the food."

"It's early yet," I said.

"Early! It's nine o'clock. I've usually filled the pans a second time by now. I've got potatoes, bacon, and sausage all ready to go for a refill."

"Don't cook any more, Pauline, or we'll be feeding everyone for free just so it doesn't go to waste."

By ten thirty things started looking up a little. The Killer Bee Motorcycle Club rolled in with about twenty-five bikers, and they were hungry and thirsty. I made sure to welcome them personally and thank them for coming.

"How was the ride?" I asked one of the guys in the group.

"Great until we got here," was his reply.

"Oh, no, what do you mean by that?"

"There are more cops out there than motorcyclists, and they're giving tickets for everything except breathing. I've never seen anything like it. They have cars and motorcycles pulled over everywhere from Highway Twenty-five on. They've got attitudes, too. 'Welcome to Hollister'—that's a laugh."

"I'm so sorry. I don't know what to say."

"Hey, it's not your fault."

"I know, but it makes me feel terrible. I knew the chief was going to pull this crap. There goes our weekend."

"He's not running us off," my patron said. "We're here for the weekend. It's a tradition with us. We're staying at Bolado Park, so you'll be seeing plenty of us."

"Thank you; I really appreciate that."

Business picked up as the day wore on. We were thrilled to see so many familiar faces. Year after year we could count on these wonderful people to make the pilgrimage to Johnny's from all over the world. Our Boozefighters came from as far away as Italy. I was so grateful for them.

The stories of the overzealous law enforcement officers just kept on coming. It wasn't just the motorcyclists they were targeting either. It was said the people in their driveways who hadn't buckled up yet and had their engine running were ticketed. It was rumored that a seventy-year-old man was ticketed for riding his bicycle on the sidewalk. Cars that had their windows tinted legally were given a citation regardless. Having a two-inch pocketknife in one's pocket was grounds for being thrown against the wall and frisked by one officer while the other five in the group stood by with hands on their nightsticks. The entire town of Hollister was being terrorized by the very people who were supposed to protect it. By five o'clock that evening the phone was ringing off the hook with people asking what the heck was going on in Hollister. The telephone rang again and I hesitantly answered it.

"Hey, I'm calling from Bakersfield," said the voice on the phone. "We were going to head up that way for the weekend, but we've been hearing all kinds of stuff about the cops out there. They say they're ticketing everybody. Is that true?"

"I'd love to say it's not, but I'm not going to lie to you. If you decide to drive up, make sure that your bike has everything in working order and that your helmet is DOT approved. Put both feet down at the stop signs, and whatever you do, don't bring a pocketknife. I'm sorry. Am I rambling here?"

"That's just the way I heard it. My brother rode up from Fresno and he said they had six people in cars and on motorcycles pulled over in a one-block radius. We wanted to come to Hollister, but not if the cops are being dicks."

"I'd love for you to come here, too. It's not a pretty picture, though. I'm so angry I can hardly see straight. If you decide to ride out anyway, you be sure and come into Johnny's and introduce yourself and I'll buy you a beer. My name is Charisse. I'm the owner here."

"If we decide to come we'll be sure to see you. Johnny's is the only reason to come out there this year."

I hung up fuming. I didn't want to let all of the BS get to me. Getting upset didn't change anything, and it put me in a foul mood. I gave lip service to trusting God, and now I needed to do it. I had just finished giving myself a pep talk when a wonderful bunch of Boozefighters came through the door.

I walked up to greet them and was surrounded by burly bikers covered in leather and tattoos who lined up for a hug. I saw some of them three or four times a year, some only during the Fourth of July weekend, and some I had never even met. There were hugs all around just the same. The love and respect these guys gave me humbled me and made me realize how much I was blessed. It was just what I needed to snap out of my funk. I wasn't going to make the money I was used to making. I'd been sending employee's home left and right and calling people who were scheduled to come in and telling them not to bother. I suggested they find a designated driver or grab a cab and come on down for a drink on me. If we weren't going to be making money we could at least be enjoying one another's company.

And that was exactly what we did. I met a wonderful Boozefighter from northern California who went by the name of Wizard. We spent hours talking about everything under the sun, and laughing. The actor Robert Patrick (*The Terminator*) was the Boozefighters Los Angeles chapter president, and he made the trek to Hollister. He was down-to-earth and a pleasure to talk to. We talked about Wino Willie and his family, Johnny's history, and, of course, law enforcement. He was kind enough to pose for pictures with me, and I was tickled pink that a famous actor was hanging out at my place and having a good time. Before I knew it the entire building was full of Boozefighters. Everywhere I looked there was green, white, and leather. I started to think that I might have sent too many employees home. The bikers were gracious and patient and everyone had a wonderful time. With time to visit I was getting to know a lot of Boozefighters better and thoroughly enjoying it.

The Un-rally of 2006

Me & Robert Patrick.

Me and Wizard.

Boozefighter & Patriot Club members.

That was the way it was for three days. I got acquainted with the greatest people. We laughed and danced to the jukebox and enjoyed hanging out together. We drank and had so much fun that my car didn't make it home all weekend. Every night I rode home with one of my bartenders. Tommy skipped going to Shasta because of the uncertainty of the weekend, and every morning he drove me back to work. The Johnny's crew agreed that even though we weren't making the kind of money we were used to, we sure were enjoying ourselves. The chief and the council may have killed our rally, but they couldn't kill our spirit. Such was the un-rally of 2006, or what came to be known as "the Law Enforcement Rally."

KITCHEN STILL SPINNING

The Fourth of July weekend came and went, and despite the financial loss I managed to stay pretty calm—for me. The city council was sure to get an earful from many of its citizens because of the weekend's law enforcement debacle. I intended to give them my two cents' worth, but first I needed to get the place back to normal. The beer I had ordered for Thursday and Friday carried me through the entire weekend and well into the following week. Where food was concerned, what we couldn't freeze, we ran as specials and gave away as happy-hour appetizers.

The next five months were a living hell where the kitchen was concerned. Juan became very unreliable and I had to let him go. The cooks I hired didn't show up and didn't call, they were arrested, or they were way too slow (never hire an employee whose nickname is Turtle). The last cook I hired in that period of time was a nice enough guy, but frankly, his food was mediocre. Our signature meals, like fajita chicken salads and Philly cheese steaks, did not taste the way they used to. Lunch sales were down about twenty-five percent, and I was at a loss about what to do. I hadn't seen even a bad applicant in months. Then one day, as I was pulling my lunch special sign in, a nice-looking young man with a buzz cut and sparkling brown eyes came through the door.

"Hi, there, is the owner here?" he asked.

"I'm the owner. What can I do for you?" I said.

"Hi, I'm Jonny. You wouldn't happen to be hiring, would you?"

"That depends on what kind of a job you're looking for. If you're a cook with some real experience, this might be your lucky day."

"As a matter of fact, I am," he said. "Here's my résumé."

I took his résumé and looked it over. "I see you went to culinary school. You've got quite a bit of experience, so why is it you aren't working right now?"

"I moved back to Washington with my parents and that didn't work out real well, so I came back to California. A friend I worked with in Gilroy has a place here, and he said if I wanted to move back, he had a place for me to stay, so here I am."

"Can you make soups from scratch?"

"Of course I can."

"Can you flip an egg? I mean without breaking the yolk. You don't know how many cooks tell me that they can flip an egg when they really can't."

"Yes, I can flip an egg. I make a mean omelet, too."

"If I hire you, you will need to make this kitchen your own. You do your own ordering, make up your own specials, and keep the kitchen tidy. I don't want another cook who needs me and Sylvia to hold his hand. That's Sylvia behind the bar. You would be working mainly with her. I'll introduce you."

I introduced Jonny to Syl as a bona fide chef who was looking for work. We were both hopeful that he would be the one to get the kitchen back on track. When he left I immediately called one of his references, and the man had nothing but good things to say about Jonny. I ran downstairs and skipped around the bar, toasting with customers as I informed them that my hell days in the kitchen were over. Needless to say, no one else shared my enthusiasm. The truest customers had stuck it out with us the previous six months, ordering only what they figured would be a safe choice off the menu. I bought quite a few lunches and cocktails for my regulars

Kitchen Still Spinning

as a way of thanking them for their loyalty. They were going to have to see this to believe it.

"Let me ask you, Charisse," one of my doubting Thomas customers said. "Exactly how many cooks have you been through this year?"

"Well, smarty pants, if you must know, quite a few. Let's see, it goes something like this: Rey left and I hired Juan. Juan didn't do very well, so I hired Henry to replace him. Henry turned out to be a flake, so I begged Juan to come back. Juan came back and missed a bunch of work because of a bad tooth and a nasty hangover so I let him go again and hired James. James got arrested, so I called Juan and begged him to come back again, and he agreed to help out until I could find someone else. He came in to replace the arrested employee wearing a T-shirt that said, 'Got Bail?' on the front of it, and Syl and I almost died laughing. He planned on staying until we found a replacement, but when he stopped at the DMV to renew his driver's license on his way to work, he found out that he had an outstanding warrant and he was arrested. Then there was the Turtle, who lived up to his nickname, and Karleen, who also wound up being a flake, followed by Bruce. Bruce was nice, but couldn't cut the mustard as our regular cook. Then in walks a man named Jonny who stopped by on a fluke and had wonderful references. I'm praying God sent him here to put an end to my misery. So there you have it. I don't blame you for being doubtful, but I have faith that better days are ahead for us at Johnny's!"

* * *

If I had not invited God back into my life, I would not have lived through 2006. My husband continued to wrestle his demons while he was remodeling our home. Remodels have been known to lead to divorce. How a newly recovering alcoholic, married to a bar owner, dealing with my stressful cook situation and the uncertainty of the canceled rally survived it was nothing short of a miracle.

* * *

The Lord truly does work in mysterious ways, and He brought Victor back into our lives. Tommy met up with him at an AA meeting and wound up becoming his sponsor. Victor was trying hard to put his life back together, but had some pretty large hurdles to conquer. For starters, he didn't have a job or a place to live. Seth and Jeannie's motor home was parked at the side of our house, and they agreed to let Victor stay in it until he got on his feet.

Without his help I don't know how long it would have taken to get the remodel finished. Tommy, still a procrastinator at heart, needed Victor's muscle as well as his momentum, and while we helped get him back on his feet, he helped us finish the daunting task of remodeling the entire front of our house. Victor eventually found a job, saved some money, and flew away from our little nest. He left as a stronger man who beat his addiction to drugs and restored his relationship with his wife and children.

Oh, what a wonderful God we serve. Opening up our home to help him was one of the most satisfying things I had ever done. However, Tommy is a very private man, so even though Victor wasn't living in the house, Tommy seemed like he was in a pretty constant state of touchiness. With everything I had on my plate, his constant complaining more than irritated me.

THE HOLLISTER MOTORCYCLE RALLY COMMITTEE

While living through all that craziness, I dove headfirst into trying to save our rally when I joined the Hollister Motorcycle Rally Committee. My good pal Robbie Scatinni was the only council member who had the sense to see what the rally meant to Hollister. He tried hard to keep it alive in 2006, but he was only one man on a five-person council. When he couldn't save the 2006 rally, he had the idea of bringing together a group of Hollister businesses and citizens that could work with a promoter to bring our rally back in 2007. He recruited me to help, and I was determined to put my money where my mouth was and help save the event that meant so much to our community and my business.

After the 2006 debacle and the embarrassment it caused, I had to get involved. I was proud to work with Robbie and the wonderful people who volunteered so much of their time and energy to keep our rally alive. I'll give you the short version of the demise of our rally. I've told the story so many times that I look forward to being able to say, "Just read the book. It's all in there."

Miracles and Grace in an Unlikely Place

The city started losing an undetermined amount of money on our motorcycle rally in 2003, the same year that Police Chief Jeff Miller was hired. Before Miller came on board the state of California's Department of Justice, Alcoholic Beverage Control, California Highway Patrol, and Probation Department sent officers free of charge to assist the Hollister Police and San Benito Cunty Sheriff Departments in policing an event that, every year on Fourth of July weekend, brought more than a hundred thousand people to Hollister.

The council members of the time and the chief will tell you that it was sheer coincidence that the city started being charged for services after Miller was hired, but there are many, myself included, who have our doubts. The chief was given an open checkbook without oversight, and costs skyrocketed. When the city got stuck with a huge bill for a lot of unwarranted law enforcement, the council had their reason for canceling the rally.

When Robbie approached me about being part of a committee to revive our motorcycle rally, I didn't hesitate to offer my full support. Some townspeople were under the impression that Johnny's was the only business in the county that made any money during the motorcycle rally, and I wanted them to know that I was willing to work hard to make it a success. The people of that opinion were not biker enthusiasts and usually left town or holed up in their homes for the duration of the event. They were, however, members of our community, and I cared about their opinion.

In my many efforts to keep our rally going over the years, I walked miles passing out surveys that addressed people's feelings about our rally, negative as well as positive. The resounding response from people who opposed the rally was that they didn't think taxpayers should bear the burden of the costs. I repeatedly told them that all of the financial benefits weren't made clear, and that without the outrageous and unnecessary law enforcement bill there would be plenty of excess money in the city's coffers in the form of permit fees, sales tax revenue, and the trickle-down funds from every business that did well during the event. The extra employees businesses hired would have more money to spend in

The Hollister Motorcycle Rally Committee

our community, and every grocery store, gas station, hotel, restaurant, and bar in the county would profit from it.

Ninety percent of the people I talked with were pro rally. They failed to understand why our city council members refused to see the benefits to our city. I begged people to fill city hall to the rafters anytime a discussion about the rally was planned, on or off of the agenda. I was always disappointed in how few business owners showed up to voice their opinion. The lack of them in attendance gave credence to the council's theory that my business was one of the very few that benefited from a rally, and it always angered me. Apathy played a huge part in bringing down our rally, and I was determined to stay involved and fight.

When I told Tommy about joining the committee, he understood why I felt that I needed to participate, but he also worried about the time I would need to invest.

"Are you sure you have the time to put into this effort?" he asked.

"It won't be easy, I know, but I have to be a part of it, honey."

"If you get the rally back, how will you find time to do committee duties and run the bar?"

"I'll tell everyone up front that I'll help until June, but then I need to walk away. That gives me almost nine months to help out. That's a lot better than nothing."

"You do what you need to do, but I hope I don't have to say, 'I told you so.'"

"I hope you don't either."

ROAD TRIP—THE STURGIS INVESTIGATION

A view of the Sturgis Rally was a lot like the Hollister Rally.

Me & Sturgis PD.

Me and Chief Bush

Miracles and Grace in an Unlikely Place

I decided that in the interest of finding out how Sturgis, maintained their rally with so much success, I would go to South Dakota and meet with key people and ask them about how things were done there. I was fully prepared to go alone, because I knew the trip would not be something Tommy would enjoy. From what we saw in Daytona I knew there weren't enough AA meetings in South Dakota to get him through another motorcycle rally.

I mentioned to a friend at Johnny's that I was going, and she said that she had always wanted to go to Sturgis and would love to tag along. Having someone to share the hotel and rental car bill with was going to make my endeavor much less expensive. I booked our flights and searched online for a hotel that was walking distance from the hub of things. I found a motel right on the main drag, and it was only blocks away from the activities. It came at premium price of $283 a night before taxes, with a minimum three-night stay, so I was thrilled to have my friend Stephanie to share the costs. We also needed a rental car, so our little excursion was going to be quite expensive. I felt it would be worth it if I could come home with information for our city council and the Hollister Motorcycle Rally Committee that would help our endeavor.

I called the Sturgis Police Department to schedule an appointment with someone in law enforcement during my visit and was delighted to find that Chief Jim Bush himself was glad to find time for me. I was surprised that a man with so much on his plate during a rally that draws more than five hundred thousand participants could work me into his schedule. I was going at the tail end of their three-week event, but I'd figured Chief Bush would be too busy. I also arranged a meeting with the Sturgis Motorcycle Rally director. As the time grew close I was more excited than ever. I knew Stephanie and I were going to have a ball while I did my research.

About two weeks before we were supposed to leave, Steph informed me that her ex-boyfriend wanted to go, too. I wasn't happy about becoming a third wheel, but when she told me that he was going to pay for her half of our room, cover the rental car costs, drive us to the airport, and cover the parking costs for his car, I realized I would benefit from his tagging along. The trip was

Road Trip—The Sturgis Investigation

stretching us both financially, so even though I wasn't really happy about the change in plans, I couldn't complain.

"Everything will be just the same," she assured me, but I knew there was no way that would be true. I had a job to do while I was there, and decided that it must be for the best.

When Steph and Ron arrived to pick me up, Tommy told him to look out for me. He wanted to know I would be safe. With all of our issues, trusting each other in the physical department was never a problem. There aren't too many men who would let their wife go off to the Sturgis Motorcycle Rally without them, and Ron as much as told Tommy so.

Ron arranged to rent a motorcycle, too, while we were in Sturgis, and Steph and I followed Ron in the rental car to the motel. When we arrived I wondered whether we had the right place. I could not believe that an establishment the equivalent of a Motel 6 in a low-rent neighborhood could charge $283 a night. Just goes to show you what a rally can do for the local economy. It was a shabby little place, but it was clean, and from what everyone told us I could indeed walk to the festivities from there.

Walking down the main street was kind of like walking down San Benito Street during our rally; it was just a much longer street. Bikes were parked on both sides of the street and down the middle. At the intersections there were barriers where police officers in shorts and T-shirts directed traffic. They were cordial and I took pictures with them to show the folks back home how an officer of the law ought to act. They smiled and made people feel welcome. I stopped and talked with quite a few of them, and they all said they enjoyed working the rally and volunteered to work it. Go figure—what was Hollister's problem?

I talked with people in the buildings on the main street and found that half were vacant all year long. Landlords made plenty of money renting their buildings out one month a year and left them vacant the rest. I met the owner of a plumbing store who told me she and her husband closed their business once a year to sell Indian bread in their store. They just moved a few things aside, and they made more money selling Indian bread and soft drinks for three weeks than they did plumbing supplies all year long.

Miracles and Grace in an Unlikely Place

Everyone I talked to could not understand how Hollister could not make a go of our rally. They all loved what the rally did for their community and figured that without it Sturgis wouldn't even be on the map. I got incensed thinking about what we were going to continue to miss out on if we didn't get our rally back on track.

After a little shopping and a lot of visiting, we made our way to one of the many bars for a beverage. The taverns were huge, most sporting a minimum of four bars to belly up to for a cocktail. Unlike in Daytona, the bartenders wore more appropriate attire. The women wore short shorts and low-cut tops, but their outfits weren't offensive.

Every bar was packed, and I was overjoyed when two seats just inside the door of the Oasis Bar & Lounge opened up as we approached. A very pleasant bartender waited on us, and after a cold one, my companions decided to scout around. I told them to go on without me, because I had found my spot. I stayed there for about two hours, people watching and visiting with hordes of bikers, before my friends returned, ready to hunt down a meal. I was treated wonderfully by everyone I met, and hated to leave. I promised the bartender that I would be back the next day.

As we headed out I thought about how many people told me the same thing about leaving Johnny's, and I swelled with pride. After dinner at a restaurant across the street from our motel, we settled in for the evening. I didn't sleep very well. The air conditioner made horrible noises. I lay there thinking about what I was paying for the rinky-dink motel room and got mad as hell at Hollister hotel owners who failed to show up at any of the city council meetings relating to the rally. *Darn lazy people*, I thought.

The Cinderella Motel was the only one ever represented at those meetings, and it was booked solid every year with Boozefighters, rally or no rally. Letty, the manager, even put on a big barbecue for them every year. Some people get it, and some people don't.

The next day, while my companions went for a motorcycle ride, I headed out for my meetings with Chief Bush and Lisa, the head of the Sturgis Rally Organization. I walked six blocks to the main street, and almost every house had motorcycles in front of them, alongside them, and anywhere they could fit them. People rented

Road Trip—The Sturgis Investigation

out their driveways for parking, and opened coffeehouses in their living rooms. I'd never seen anything like it. Something like that would never take place in California. Our bureaucrats would make sure there were way too many hoops to jump through for people to capitalize on the situation.

While downtown I ran into my travel companions, and we had a fantastic breakfast before I headed off to my meetings. Everyone we met up with was cordial and helpful, and I got directions to the police station and the rally office from one of the locals.

* * *

The police station was just blocks away in a two-story building. Chief Bush was a tall, nice-looking man with an easygoing demeanor. I was comfortable with him right away, and he was helpful and answered all of my questions. He reiterated what the officers I spoke with told me about volunteering for the job a year in advance. I told him how ridiculous I thought it was that our chief managed to run up a law enforcement bill for more than $300,000 for a three-day event, and he pointed out that his guys were getting paid about $16 an hour, compared to California's $50 to $60 an hour. He told me it was like comparing apples to oranges, and said that California also had a lot more regulatory hoops to jump through, as well as different workers' comp criteria.

I told him how much I admired the attitudes of his officers. They were in groups of two, smiling and laughing, compared to our surly eight-man squads who acted like they'd just as soon arrest you as look at you. He assured me that he had as many men on the street as we did, but that many were undercover. That made sense to me. The chances of catching the bad guys have got to improve when you aren't advertising that you're a cop.

"I sure wish you could have a talk with our chief," I told him. "I can see that your men have a great attitude because of you. I don't know why our chief is so antibiker, but his attitude has certainly been passed on to his men. Most of them wouldn't know congenial if it hit them upside the head."

Miracles and Grace in an Unlikely Place

"Give your chief a break," he told me. "He's got a lot to deal with. You've got your Hells Angels and Mongols out there, and we have the Angels, Outlaws, and Banditos out here. It's all very serious business."

"From what I can see, you're handling it beautifully. If I could get you a paid trip to Hollister, would you come out and talk to our chief and city council?"

"I've always wanted to go to California. As long as it didn't interfere with hunting season I'd love to go. We take deer season seriously around here, too."

We shook hands before I left, but I felt more like giving him a hug. He was such a nice, unpretentious man. He gave me his card and told me to call anytime I had questions. I left determined to find a way to get him to Hollister to talk to our local government.

The Sturgis rally office was only a couple of blocks away from the police department in another two-story building. Lisa Weyer, the rally director, was also very gracious with her time and counsel. She loaded me down with maps, brochures, and lots of information to take back to Hollister. She, too, said that she'd never been to California and would love joining the chief there if I arranged a trip. They obviously had a sound relationship.

I left her office and made my way back to my new favorite watering hole in Sturgis. When I got to the Oasis, lo and behold there was one seat at the bar waiting for me. My little bartender wasn't there, but an equally pleasant gal was in her place. I introduced myself and ordered a Miller Lite.

"Kathy told me that you would probably be coming back today and said that I should take good care of you."

"All the people passing through this bar and she told you to look out for me?"

"She said you owned a bar in Hollister, that you were real nice and a good tipper. We take care of the folks who take care of us."

"Well, I really appreciate it."

Unlike in Daytona, in Sturgis everyone knew about Hollister. They didn't necessarily know about Johnny's, but they knew about our rally. There was one man at the bar who looked familiar to me. I tried not to stare, but I was sure I had seen him before. He was with a group who seemed very comfortable at the bar and knew everyone. There was one woman in the bunch and she was hanging all over most of the men. She had on a see-through mesh shirt with nothing on underneath but pasties. As she moved from one end of the bar to the other draping herself all over men, I said to the bartender in a whisper, "I throw broads like that out of my place."

Just about then the man I thought I recognized walked up to me and said, "You're the owner of Johnny's in Hollister, aren't you?"

"Yes, I am. I thought I recognized you, and it was driving me crazy. Do you come to Hollister for our rally?"

"I live in Gilroy," he told me. "I never miss the Hollister Rally."

"I knew you looked familiar," I said.

He told me his name and then, pointing to the lady I had pegged as loose, said, "You remember my wife?"

It was all I could do to keep my mouth from hitting the floor. The bartender turned her back to me immediately and was laughing into her hand. I have no idea how I kept a straight face, or even whether I did, as I held my hand out to shake hers. Luckily my Gilroy friend went about introducing me to everyone else and explaining the significance of Hollister and Johnny's.

Suddenly I had a delightful group of people to party with. I wound up spending hours at the bar people watching, and when Steph called to see how I was doing I told her she could find me right where we were the previous evening. She and Ron left the bike at the motel and drove the car so that they could give me a ride home after we checked out the nightlife. By the time they arrived I was quite tipsy and very hungry. After introductions we asked about a good place to eat dinner. As it turned out, many of them were hungry, too, so Gilroy, his wife and a couple others took us to one of their favorite spots and we all had dinner together. While we were enjoying our meal I found that when Gilroy's wife wasn't hanging on other men, she seemed like a pretty normal person who genuinely cared for her husband. To each his own, I guess.

It was great having guides, and we got to see out-of-the-way places that a tourist might not ever find. It was the wildest thing

I had ever seen. People opened bars in their garages that backed up to alleyways. When they wanted to close they just pulled down the garage door. South Dakota was definitely looser with liquor licenses than California.

As it was in Daytona, bar crowds swelled to four times their normal size, and every parking lot and alleyway became a part of the bars. Amazingly, with all the craziness I didn't see any cops. With the chief's assurance that there were plenty of undercover guys around, I assumed that they could have been just about anyone.

As the evening wore on, people got more intoxicated, the music got louder and wilder, and I decided it was time for me to call it a night. Fortunately my companions felt the same way. They gave me no argument about heading back to the hotel. With all the beer in my system I slept like a log, and never even heard the loud air conditioner.

The next morning we took off early for Deadwood, Mount Rushmore, and the Crazy Horse Memorial. There wasn't much to see in Deadwood, and Mount Rushmore was inspiring, but Crazy Horse was the hit of the trip. It was even more majestic than Rushmore to me, not just because all four heads of Rushmore would fit into Crazy Horse's head, but because of the story behind it.

For sixty years the Ziolkowski family of sculptors has worked on the monument in the Black Hills with funding from donations and tour charges only. The memorial is a private, nonprofit undertaking that has refused government funds. Korczak, the original sculptor, died in 1982, leaving his wife, Ruth, and their ten children to carry on the dream. Ruth is the president and CEO of the Crazy Horse Memorial Foundation, and when she shares her husband's passion for the monument, you can't help but be inspired. It was an experience I'll never forget, and I'd say anyone who left there without being moved and fired up about the American spirit would have to be comatose.

* * *

It rained hard on the way back to Sturgis, and I felt terrible for all the soaking-wet riders we passed. I guess that's the chance you

Road Trip—The Sturgis Investigation

take when you go to Sturgis; you never know about the weather. It made me wonder why the state of California's tourism industry didn't wake up to the potential of our rally. With San Francisco, Monterey, Big Sur, and Santa Cruz only hours away from Hollister, and our great weather, we would be an easy sell if they got on the bandwagon.

We stopped by the Full Throttle Saloon on the way home and I was blown away. I counted twenty-six bars, and it's possible that I missed a couple. It was the tail end of the rally and things were winding down, but there were still lots of biker activities going on and plenty of bars open. The bartenders were dressed in bikinis with chaps, and from what I was told they came in from all over the country to work the rally just for tips. It was a little wild for my taste, but it was something else to experience.

With a suitcase full of information, a pile of T-shirts, and ankles the size of my calves, I headed home. I was glad to have had the experience, but ready to be back in my nice quiet house with my husband and my cats. I had one day of downtime before throwing myself fully into the rally committee, and I looked forward to sharing all that I had seen with my fellow rally enthusiasts.

THE 2007 AND 2008 HOLLISTER MOTORCYCLE RALLIES

Some favorite Boozefighters

The 2007 and 2008 Hollister Motorcycle Rallies

Jeana & Kat working hard.

Sylvia and Annie are pooped.

Miracles and Grace in an Unlikely Place

Despite never having been on a committee, I wound up being the Hollister Motorcycle Rally chairperson. It was a real eye-opener and learning experience for me. Our first job was to find a promoter. Our job didn't just entail picking someone we thought we could work with; the city council had to like him, too. We came to believe that Seth Doulton of Horse Power Promotions was the man for the job. His company was the smallest in the bidding, but it seemed that he was genuine about keeping us, our rally, and our city's best interests at the forefront. Once he was on board, we discussed the presentation for the city council that would get our plan approved and start the ball rolling for a 2007 motorcycle rally. Many great ideas were hatched, plenty of nonprofits were involved, and we believed that we could close the deal with the council. I had the job of delivering a presentation that would wow the council—so much for not wanting to speak publicly—and I worked diligently on it for more than a month.

I had the idea of adding a venue for Christian motorcycle enthusiasts, because as far as I knew, no other motorcycle rally did so, but it never came to pass. There are thousands of Christian motorcycle clubs in all fifty states and abroad, and I still believe we missed a golden opportunity. I've learned to pick my battles, and getting the rally back on track was job one.

With the help of a city council member on board, a promoter the council seemed to like, and a ton of prayer, the Hollister Motorcycle Rally Committee got the go-ahead to put on the 2007 rally. I was ecstatic, but the work had just begun. We met weekly, and some meetings went on for more than an hour and a half because my lack of experience kept me from keeping meetings in order. Seth finally gave me a gavel, and when ten people started talking at the same time I could bring a little order to the meeting by pounding it on the table. God bless each and every one of those dedicated volunteers. They all had the best intentions, but many times I left the meetings exhausted and in need of a stiff drink.

* * *

The 2007 and 2008 Hollister Motorcycle Rallies

The biggest change to the venue was moving the bikes off of San Benito Street. Seth did it for two reasons: first and foremost, to placate the chief and reduce law enforcement costs. Second, logistically it was easier that way to get power and water to the vendors, and therefore saved money. I enjoyed not breathing in the exhaust fumes, but the majority of the attendees wanted the motorcycles back on San Benito Street, and many likened the new arrangement to a flea market.

We worked hard for months, but I was able to attend only a few of the final meetings in June because my hands were full. The committee and Seth arranged for two bandstands and beer gardens, numerous vendors, famous bike builders, and biker games, and the movies *The Wild One* and *Easy Rider* played at our local theater for hours each day.

Despite the fact that attendees were well behaved, around eleven thirty on Friday and Saturday nights, Johnny's once again became the place for hordes of law enforcement officers to hang out, giving revelers the stink eye. There were a few with decent dispositions. I wished our officers had the great attitudes of the cops in Sturgis who got only a third of the pay and yet enjoyed themselves. I'll always believe their leader sets the tone.

* * *

For months while I worked on the committee, my husband went off to AA meetings and I attended rally meetings. It seemed like we hardly saw each other, and when we did, we fell asleep on the couch watching TV. He was making tremendous strides in his walk with God, and even though my spiritual time was minimal, I can honestly say that God is the only reason I stayed sane. He taught me many lessons through the experience about keeping my mouth shut, as well as showing people grace. I am proud of what the rally committee accomplished that year, and I think I am a better person for the experience, but I won't be signing up for another committee anytime soon.

* * *

Miracles and Grace in an Unlikely Place

I felt like the 2007 rally went well, and when it was over, the committee and Seth managed to cover the outlandish $330,000 law enforcement bill. Many nonprofits made a lot of money they desperately needed, and many businesses had extra money in their coffers for a rainy day. I was thrilled that we had succeeded, but it was a harrowing experience for me, so when the San Benito County Chamber of Commerce offered take over in 2008, I couldn't have been happier. I believed that our local chamber of commerce as well as the Hollister Downtown Association should have been behind the rally all along, and I prayed they would do a good job. Committee members were assured that our help would be needed, and the volunteers' phone numbers were passed on to the chamber. I was actually thrilled when my phone didn't ring, but apparently no one's did.

Somewhere along the line, instead of accepting a $100,000 contract for the T-shirt sales—which was $85,000 less than the committee negotiated the previous year—the powers that be (it's still debated as to who that was) and Seth decided that the city should take over T-shirt sales in an effort to make more money. It was a really bad idea. I told everyone who would listen that it was a terrible idea. I'm just a little bar owner, and I contract out my T-shirt sales during the rally because it's just too much. Suffice it to say that after a $98,000 loss on T-shirts that year, the city had a bad taste left in its mouth for the rally. Top that with the chief jacking up the law enforcement bill again, and we were doomed. Despite the fact that Seth moved the rally out a weekend to help lower the law enforcement bill, further upsetting attendees, costs still skyrocketed to $356,000. Hello! Did anyone see a recurring problem here?

I pleaded at city council meetings for the city manager and council to tell the chief to ease up during the Fourth of July weekend and stop spending unwarranted city funds. At many of the meetings I was the only business owner to step up to the podium. Speaking in public still made my stomach tie up in knots and my hands shake, but if something is important enough to you, you press past your fear. Some people attended the meetings to show their support, but when they didn't speak, it didn't matter that they were there.

The 2007 and 2008 Hollister Motorcycle Rallies

Whether it was fear or apathy, without enough outcries from the community, our council didn't have the backbone to move forward. If they told the chief to cut back on law enforcement—say, only one helicopter, and cops in packs of four instead of eight—and something went wrong, they would be held accountable. Despite twelve successful rallies without a major incident, it was a losing battle, and once again the rally was canceled.

STILL GROWING

TRUST AND MOUTH ISSUES CONTINUE

After the rally cancellation I was a very angry woman. I wanted to give up, face the fact that our rally was a done deal, stop complaining about it, and move on. It was hard. In a down economy we needed the extra funds. Every year I counted on the post-rally money I stashed to get us through the leaner times. Without the rally I knew our savings would shrink, and I was scared about not having money put away for a rainy day. I grew up struggling financially. I got weird about not having my safety net. I knew that God wanted me to lean on Him and trust that He had my back. How many times had He already proved it to me?

I needed to look at the positive side of things. Many Boozefighters enjoyed Hollister more without a rally, because they had free rein at Johnny's. No line to get in the door, easy access to the bartenders, and lightning-fast service all made their visit more enjoyable. I benefited from the situation, too. With more time to spend with my Boozefighter friends, I was getting to know them better than ever.

Trust and Mouth Issues Continue

Me and Dago.

Me, Vern Autry and Dago

Miracles and Grace in an Unlikely Place

Me with Boozefighters and some of the original Top Hatters infront of our famous mural.

Dago, the last living original Boozette, became one of my closest friends. Wino Willie's wife, Terrie, was her riding buddy back in the day. Dago joined the club when she was sixteen years old. She has the memory of an elephant, and plenty of stories to share. She is eighty-two, has survived two bouts of cancer, and is tough as nails. I started enjoying Boozefighter conventions as her roomie, and we amassed more stories. I got to know Vern Autry, a Boozefighter who rode to Hollister in 1947 on his Shovelhead. He filled me in on details about 1947 that I would never have known without his friendship. I'm a writer with a historic bar. What could be better?

* * *

Despite coming a long way spiritually, I still had trust and mouth issues. I continued to worry, grumble, and complain about

Trust and Mouth Issues Continue

our financial woes. I was thrilled that Tommy was sober, but he still had very little work, and now I was irritated about how much money he spent on coffee and ice cream. I'd stopped thanking God for my husband's sobriety and was now asking Him to send him work and make him more conscientious about money. Here I was again, looking at the glass as half-empty, seeing my lack instead of rejoicing in my blessings. How many times would I have to go around the same mountain? Would I ever learn to trust God and keep my mouth shut?

I had Jonny, a good cook whom everyone loved and who was like a son to me. My customers were being more considerate about their language, and business was going as well as could be expected during a recession. I had so much to be thankful for, and I was appreciative, but at the same time I constantly worried about finances.

And I worried about the fact that Tommy didn't share my zeal for growing spiritually. Once again I wanted things done my way and in my timing, and once more God used my husband to show me that I was not the one in control. To use a Joyce-ism, I needed to let my husband off of the potter's wheel. I also needed to be more grateful for the changes that had already taken place in our lives.

If I was really going to leave Tommy to God, it would entail zipping my lip, an issue that still challenged me. Listening to one of Joyce's teaching tapes, *Me and My Big Mouth,* and reading her book of the same title helped me tremendously. As I saturated myself in her teachings and prayed more about my issues, I paid less and less attention to what Tommy was doing. I was finally learning to leave him to God, and I was getting real good at stuffing it. I think that's exactly what God wanted me to do: shut up and get the heck out of His way. As usual, once I did He worked His miracles.

* * *

I'd gone to the Joyce Meyer women's conference in Saint Louis to get my spiritually drained tank refilled, and left Tommy home to his own devices. We talked every night and morning, as we always did while apart. I was at the airport in Dallas waiting for

Miracles and Grace in an Unlikely Place

my plane to San Jose when Tommy called me. He told me that he had gone to my church with his friend Jimmy, and that they both had enjoyed it tremendously, music and all. When he told me that the two of them planned on going the following week, my heart soared. I'd wanted so badly for my husband to join me in church. Church is a family affair, and I always felt a void when I went alone. I was ecstatic, and couldn't wait to get home and see my husband.

NEW BEGINNINGS

Tommy and I always loved each other, even when we were unintentionally causing each other liberal amounts of pain. My codependency fed off of his alcoholism, and his alcoholism fed off of my codependency. It is only by the grace of God that we both came to address our issues and remain married and in love. With God's help we have a healthy love for each other. It's a love with respect and admiration at its core. It is solid, and I believe with God's help we can get through anything life throws our way.

With Christ in the center of our lives, we see things differently. There are so many homeless people in Hollister. Before God's influence, when they sat on the bench outside of the bar my first thought was, *That's not good for business.* Now I view them with sympathetic eyes and I do what I can to help. While serving at the homeless shelter I find myself face-to-face with the very same people I shooed off of my bench or threw out of the bar. I am still bothered when a homeless person wants to spend the only money that he or she has on beer, but now I understand that alcoholism is an all-consuming disease. It is the only addiction that can kill you if not detoxed correctly. Coming down off of heroin will make you feel like you are going to die, but alcohol withdrawal may very well do it. You only have to ask Tommy, who was taken to the emergency room three times while in treatment with professional help to detox.

The same man who didn't care about anything but his next drink now plays the guitar for the worship team at our church and is very active with the Homeless Coalition. The husband I begged to stop using the F-word calls me potty-mouth if I say "damn." He is more committed to God than I ever dreamed possible.

Tommy is still a procrastinator, and I still have my control issues and would prefer that he get started on things sooner than he does. But more often than not these days we meet somewhere in the middle. And that's what marriage is about: meeting in the middle and giving each other room to be who God wants us to be.

I believe it's part of His divine plan. I find that most couples are polar opposites. God in his infinite wisdom arranged it that way, so that we can complement each other while helping each other to grow. A little heads-up here: We never stop growing, and we're never perfect. We only need to give God our best efforts. 2 Chronicles 16:9 says, "For the eyes of the Lord search back and forth across the whole earth, looking for people whose hearts are perfect toward Him, so that He can show His great power in helping them." He continues to amaze me, and I believe He's just getting started.

EPILOGUE

I'm so grateful that God gives us a clean slate every day when we are truly repentant. As long as I was hanging on to all of that old baggage of self-reproach I was no good to anyone, including myself. You can't give away what you don't have, and the first step toward loving others is learning to love yourself, with all of your flaws and iniquities. I am a work in progress, and my goal in life is to become more Christlike every day.

I meet a lot more people who don't know Christ sitting on one of my bar stools than I ever will in church, and I have the awesome privilege of being used by God right where I am. It is the greatest joy of my life. Whether it's consoling someone who has lost a loved one, feeding the homeless, or being a compassionate ear for another codependent who swears she's through being mistreated, nothing is more fulfilling than getting outside of myself to be there for someone else. The opportunities present themselves daily.

My prayer is that in sharing these stories about my life—the good times and the bad, the parties and the commiseration—someone out there who is wondering whether there isn't a little bit more to life than what he or she is experiencing will give Jesus a try.

Whether you are like me—you gave your heart to Christ and then walked away—or maybe you've never given Him a chance, there is no better life than one with God at the helm.

It's possible you're thinking, *I didn't buy this book to be preached to.* Regardless of your reason for picking it up, it's in your hands now, and I hope that God will speak something into everyone's life who reads it.

I believe that God had this very purpose in mind when He allowed me to buy Johnny's. My journey in life led up to this very moment. There are thousands of addicts and alcoholics in the world, with just as many codependent enablers who have convinced themselves that they are only trying to help. It wasn't until God opened my eyes to my own issues that I was able to be of any help to my husband. He got me to shut my mouth and leave Tommy in His very capable hands, but it didn't happen overnight. He used Tommy's disease to do work in me long before He worked on my husband.

It was very painful at times. It was hard admitting my faults. I am thankful God works on our issues a little at a time. He doesn't ask us to change all of our bad behavior at once, because none of us could handle that. The person He is helping me to become is someone I'd much rather see looking back at me in the mirror. Am I perfect? Far from it. As Joyce says, "I'm not where I need to be, but thank God I'm not where I used to be."

Running a bar as a Christian is challenging. I long to write full-time and hope to someday sell Johnny's to someone who will appreciate its place in history and the important role it plays in our community. That, too, will be in God's timing.

Johnny's Bar & Grill has served me well for seventeen years. The wonderful people it brought into my life have an indelible place in my heart. God has been so good to me.

After a four-year drought, a rally revival is on the horizon, which can only mean great things for the Johnny's family. The stories just keep coming, and I can't begin to tell them all in one book.

ACKNOWLEDGEMENTS

It would take volumes to thank the people that have touched and enriched my life at Johnny's over the years. A heartfelt thank you to the wonderful customers and friends that made Johnny's more like a home than a business. I will cherish you always.

To the wonderful employees that made it possible for me to thrive in the bar business for more than seventeen years, I couldn't have done it without you and you are invaluable to me. To Annie who has become such an integral part of the team, you are a miracle and we appreciate you.

To my Boozefighter friends who are too numerous to mention, I value the relationship with the club more than I can say. Your place in Johnny's history and your determination to keep it alive means the world to all of us.

I'm grateful for Dago's rich tales and the pictures to go along with them. They fueled the flame to share my stories and I look forward to writing her biography one day.

I'm so grateful to my mother for introducing me to Christ at an early age and teaching me to be a person of integrity.

Thank you to all of my prayer warriors who gave me the strength to hang on when I didn't think I had it in me.

Thank you to my editor Marla Miller whose clear grasp of what I wanted to say helped me turn a jumbled book into a cohesive story.

To Joyce Meyer, she has no idea who I am but she impacted my life in more ways than I can say. In her straightforward fashion she helped me to grow up spiritually so that I could live the life that God had planned for me. God used her to open my eyes which made this story possible. I shared her quotes the way I remembered them. They are not verbatim.

The support of my son Allen who believes that his mamma can do just about anything is priceless.

Thank you Jesus, You are so good.

www.ingramcontent.com/pod-product-compliance
Lightning Source LLC
Chambersburg PA
CBHW071651090426
42738CB00009B/1492